GOD'S GIFT TO WOMEN

GOD'S GIFT TO WOMEN

ERIC LUDY

Multnomah Books

GOD'S GIFT TO WOMEN
published by Multnomah Books

Published in association with Loyal Arts Literary Agency, LoyalArts.com

© 2003 by Winston and Brooks, Inc.

International Standard Book Number: 1-59052-272-9

Cover image by Creatas.com

Unless otherwise indicated, Scripture quotations are from the *Revised Standard Version Bible*
© 1946, 1952 by the Division of Christian Education of the National Council of the
Churches of Christ in the United States of America.

Other Scripture quotations are from:

The Holy Bible, New International Version (NIV) © 1973, 1984 by International Bible
Society, used by permission of Zondervan Publishing House.

The Holy Bible, New King James Version (NKJV) © 1984 by Thomas Nelson, Inc.

Holy Bible, New Living Translation (NLT) © 1996. Used by permission of Tyndale House
Publishers, Inc. All rights reserved.

Published in the United States by WaterBrook Multnomah, an imprint of The Doubleday
Publishing Group, a division of Random House Inc., New York.

MULTNOMAH and its mountain colophon are registered trademarks of Random House Inc.

Printed in the United States of America

For information:
MULTNOMAH BOOKS

12265 ORACLE BOULEVARD, SUITE 200 • COLORADO SPRINGS, CO 80921
Library of Congress Cataloging-in-Publication Data

Ludy, Eric.
    God's gift to women / by Eric Ludy.
        p. cm.
Includes bibliographical references.
    ISBN 1-59052-272-9 (pbk.)
    1. Young men—Religious life. 2. Masculinity—Religious aspects—
Christianity. 3. Man-woman relationships—Religious aspects—Christianity.
I. Title.

BV4541.3.L83 2003
248.8'32—dc22

2003014365

09 10—10 9 8 7 6

To my sweet Leslie,
may I be to you everything written here.

Contents

III
FORGING THE WARRIOR

IV
SHAPING THE POET

A Note from the Author

wonder how many people will pick up this book, turn it over and look at my face on the back cover, and mutter, "If *that* is God's gift to women, then I feel sorry for femininity!" First, let me assure you that just because my name appears under the title and my picture is on the book, I am in no way claiming to be God's gift to women. In fact, I have always felt like quite the opposite. I recall a recurring nightmare in which I am ushered out in front of an enormous mob of scrutinizing females. They carefully look me over like a grocer examining a new supply of tomatoes. Then with one voice they cry out in disgust, "Sick!"

What kind of guy comes up with a lightning-rod title like *God's Gift to Women?* Not a very smart one! After all, the title has male ego written all over it. The fact that it was finally chosen as the title is ironic, because this book couldn't be further removed from stereotypical male arrogance. I would even go so far as to say that the message is the polar *opposite* of male superiority. It's a kiss on femininity's cheek. The book is written for men, but the message is truly designed to be a gift to womanhood.

I am a huge fan of femininity. Right before I started writing this book, I spent seven months assisting my wife, Leslie, in writing her book on femininity, *Authentic Beauty*. At one point along the way I became so excited about why and how God designed women that I stood up in a coffee shop and blurted out, "This is so amazing for us women to hear!"

I took a break from Leslie's book at that point, went straight to the gym, and didn't shave for a couple weeks to prove to myself that I could still grow facial hair.

But the long and short of it is, I'm not a guy that's all hyped about grunting and giving off foul odors. I'm a guy that is passionate about men being *true* men. And I'm convinced that true manhood, polished by the hand of God, is nothing short of an awe-inspiring gift to womanhood.

Contrary to the vibe that a title like *God's Gift to Women* gives off, this book is not merely about how men can more effectively relate to women. I believe that we, as men, can never *hope* to become a gift to women until we understand and accept a complete vision of Christ-built manhood.

We live in a generation of burpin'-and-scratchin' male mediocrity. Most modern-day examples of manhood are self-serving, perverted, and depraved. And we are accepting this second-rate version of masculinity into our marriages, our families, and our lives. I believe we need a new standard for masculinity—a standard that is not shaped by our culture, but by the very person of Jesus Christ. That standard is the core of this book's message.

If you were hoping for a book about relating to women, don't worry—that subject is covered thoroughly in the upcoming pages. But to learn to effectively relate to women, we must first learn to effectively relate to the *Creator* of women—Jesus Christ. We must learn the world-altering secrets of Christ-built manhood.

Manhood is a gargantuan topic. To cover it entirely is like trying to de-weed the potato fields of southern Idaho. This book does not pretend to be exhaustive on the subject of masculinity. The adventure of world-altering manhood goes far beyond the dirt trail provided in the pages of this simple book. This book offers but a starting point, the egg from which greatness is hatched. For those who want to go deeper and understand the biblical roots of this message, a biblical study guide is available on our website at www.ericandleslie.com/warriorpoet.

Now as we set out to explore God's spectacular design for manhood, I invite you to join me on the journey. This book is a sports coupe with two seats—I sit in one seat, and the second seat is crafted to perfectly fit a young man. If you are not a young man, you are certainly welcome to join me on this journey. The ride may not be as comfortable, due to the fact that this message was not designed with you in mind.

However, I'm confident that you will find the adventure both satisfying and exhilarating.

You will meet real-life people that I have encountered in my travels or during my growing-up years. Only a handful of the people I refer to have been given their real names. Since I feel it is critical that I represent modern manhood in an honest and authentic fashion, I also felt that it was necessary to protect the identities of those who will assist me. I hope to honor those who read this book and not speak disparagingly of anyone. As a result, some of my characters are creative blends of two, sometimes three, people from my life, allowing me to communicate the reality of our culture without tagging any recognizable individuals as "guilty."

I grew up a people pleaser. Yet I think it would be safe to say that this book is hardly people-pleasing. It is a message of fathomless hope, but it is also a message that can easily stir defensiveness. I remind you that the great oaks of God's kingdom are not made in the shade, but in the driving rains, the gusting winds, and the blustery chill of the open air. This message may cause you to wince, but my prayer is that the pain will lead you to a vision of world-altering manhood.

I'm confident that great manhood will once again emerge in this world, and I sense it will be in my generation. I see a fire in the eyes of many of today's young men. I hear an eagerness in their voices and in their e-mails that hungers for something more. Many books have been written on manhood, and many conferences and programs have been offered. It seems manhood is ready to be remade. But there is still something missing. It's like we, as men, finally have the powerful truck with the Hemi-magnum engine, but we don't yet have the gasoline to make the hulk move. I believe that this message, in all its simplicity, holds the fuel to make the hulk move. It holds the acorn of truth that produces the strong and intrepid oak tree. It holds the fiery pressure that squeezes the coal of masculinity into the priceless treasure of Christ-built manhood. It holds the secret to what makes men great.

The secret of manhood is one ripe with possibilities. Once planted within the masculine soul, it can mold princes from the earthen clay of peasantry, soldiers from the ash of timidity, and great lovers from the raw lumber of mere men. Manhood fashioned by the rugged carpenter's hand of God is the strength of warriors, the inspiration of poets, the wonderment of kings, the playmate of little children, and one of the greatest of God's gifts to women.

I

MANHOOD
LOST

1

The Burpers and Scratchers

Our Generation's Fruitless Attempts at Manhood

ric Ludy. I always thought it was sort of a funny name. My first name, Eric, sounded sort of like something a little bearded elf would call his pet frog. I used to dream of being a Steve or a Scott. For some reason, those names seemed to have more manly flair than Eric. My dad used to tell me that I was named after the great conqueror, Eric the Red. That made me feel somewhat better. All in all, Eric was an acceptable first name. It was the last name, *Ludy,* that posed serious threats to my coolness.

Throughout my puberty-stricken and collegiate years, no one ever called me by my first name. It was always, "Hey, Ludy!" Actually it was usually, "Hey, Lugy!", "Hey, Quaalude!", or "Hey, Looney Tunes!" I longed for a last name like Cruise, or Jordan, or even Schwarzenegger. I fantasized about how cool I would be if only I had been named Scott Schwarzenegger.

As many "mom types" have informed me throughout my life, I'm a little on the skinny side. I always hated that word, *skinny*. It evokes images of emaciated frames and bloated bellies. I think the word *trim* sounds much better. So to put it less harshly, I have always been *trim*. My mom used to say, "Well, Eric, you're just not built like a football player...uh, how can I say this, Son? You are built more like...a golfer!"

How many boys set out in life to develop a *golfer's* physique? The guys *I* looked up to during my pubertized years were tall, built like football linebackers, and able to shave a lot more than mere fuzz off their upper lips.

The wonderful season of puberty struck me much later than it was supposed to. I put in my request for it at the age of thirteen, thinking, *Okay, I'm just going to get this weird thing over with.* But it didn't come. My buddy Brent was sporting a full beard and sprouting chest hairs in the seventh grade, while in the boy's locker room I still looked like a five-foot-tall baby's bottom.

I'm thirty-two as I write this book. Even now, I still can't grow a normal-looking beard—it's patchy like a diseased lawn. It's actually quite disgusting. But I keep rather clean shaven to cover up that fact. Leslie, my wife, wonders what I would have done if I had been Amish and required to grow a beard when I married her. It's a mental image she finds rather amusing. I never laugh.

To many people's surprise, I've been lifting weights since I was twelve. People seem to think that I shouldn't lift heavy items. "Hey, Bruce, why don't you help that young man over there trying to lift up that toaster; I don't want him to hurt himself!" are the kind of statements that have haunted me throughout my life.

I like to say I have "hidden" muscles—you have to look really hard to find them. My friend Tim has often said, "Even after looking hard, you still can't find them, man!" Such is the plight of my golfer's physique.

When I was seventeen, I had two goals in life. I wanted, first of all, to be a man that all my buddies would admire. But running a close second, and sometimes stealing first position, was the desire to be a man that girls would fall over themselves to be with. I went to elaborate lengths to accomplish my two goals. It wasn't easy being skinny and "hairless," but necessity is the mother of invention. Where I fell short in physique, I attempted to make up for in romance.

One chilly autumn evening in the heart of October, I embarked upon a daring attempt to gain some female admiration. As our football team was warming up, I took my place in the bleachers, just beneath a gaggle of cute girls. I cleared my throat and waited for someone to recognize me. Finally, my buddy Randy, who wished he had the guts to do it himself, announced, "Everyone shut up! Ludy's gonna sing!"

The girls turned their gaze away from the sweaty football players on the sidelines, and I caught their rapt attention with my smoldering, squinty eyes. I launched into song.

As I reached the climax, my voice cracked with emotion. "And now I look into your eyes," I sang with raspy romance in my voice, "I can see forever. The search is over—you were with me all the while. Doo dee doodoo doo dee doodoo."

I went home later that night and realized my fly was open.

No matter how hard I tried to become God's gift to women, I was either a joke that bombed or just a skinny guy with a "good personality."

When I was nineteen and a freshman in college, a studly senior named Jared Braden asked me to do him a favor on Valentine's Day. Jared was dating Brianne Henderson, the hottest girl in Spokane, Washington.

"Ludy," he conspiratorially whispered. "I'm doing a treasure hunt for Brianne. I'm going to give her a clue that will lead her to the HUB. When she gets there, could you serenade her with that one Journey song you always sing? I've got Darrell Lufken to play the piano and everything."

I gulped. Sing for Brianne Henderson? My brain seemed to fill up with some sort of numbing agent. Like, *really* sing a love song to Brianne Henderson? After a few brain-frozen moments, I finally thawed enough to nervously chatter, "Um, okay…what time do you want me there?"

After carefully checking my zipper, I serenaded Brianne Henderson with an amorous rendition of my favorite Journey love song, "Faithfully." Everything went so well that I couldn't wait to tell my buddy Troy and win some male approval points. Later that night I had my chance to brag. Troy and I were standing next to his red pickup in the pitch-black freshman dorm parking lot. We were getting ready to go lift weights and act tough—manly cover for the fact that we were both dateless on Valentine's Day.

While Troy searched for his keys, I cleared my throat and prepared to raise myself to a new level of respect in his eyes. With a rough, gravelly voice, as if it were a piece of normal everyday news, I muttered, "I just serenaded Brianne Henderson!"

"You *what?*" Troy stammered, stopping cold in the middle of unlocking the car door.

"I just sang 'Faithfully' to Brianne Henderson!" As I repeated the words, I accidentally smiled, eroding a little of my tough nonchalance. But it was so dark out that I was hoping Troy didn't pick it up.

"Brianne Henderson? *The* Brianne Henderson?" Troy stuttered as if he had just been told that his parents were really undercover CIA operatives. "What was it like?" he eagerly questioned, abandoning any attempt to unlock his door.

We stood in the inky black night as I told him my amazing tale. At times during the animated tale, I lost complete control of my manly front and chuckled with delight like a little schoolboy. But Troy was so baffled by my story that he seemed to overlook the wimpiness with which I shared it.

"Brianne Henderson is s*ooo* gorgeous!" I declared loudly, and then I'll never forget the moment immediately following. It was like time stood still and slapped me for my stupidity. Four feet away, waiting for me to stop yammering, was none other than Brianne Henderson.

There was an awkward silence. "Uh, could you guys help me find Jared's car?" she asked uncomfortably. "Um, the riddle says that it's parked here somewhere."

I would have been better off that night singing with my fly down.

~

Manhood for me was always just out of reach. I mean, look at the raw materials God gave me to work with! What kind of manhood can you build with what I was given? I had a weak-sounding name. I was skinny from the age of two. Still to this day I have only a *single* chest hair protruding from my golfer-sized chest cavity. I was never really *great* at anything. I was always a decent athlete, but not nearly amazing enough to strike fear in the opposing team. I never stood out.

I didn't kiss a girl until I was sixteen years, seven months, and fourteen days old. And even then I slobbered down her chin, in an unsuccessful attempt to duplicate the way Sean Connery kissed as James Bond. Maybe I wasn't disgusting to women, but I would never have been picked out from among a mob of males as the most eligible bachelor.

Average. That is the best way to describe me growing up. There was nothing blatantly terrible about me, but certainly nothing ultraexciting.

Amidst the confusing fog of growing up in this modern world, like every young male, I longed to become a man. Sure, my idea of real manhood was a bit twisted and upside down. But nonetheless, I longed to be something more than just mediocre; I wanted to be a great hero among a crowd of cheering men and an object of desire to a breathless throng of women.

So what was missing? Could my problems be solved by taking some weight-gain powder, stapling a bear skin to my chest, or at least learning how not to slobber on a girl when making out? If I learned to talk tough, walk tough, and look tough, would that compensate for the missing manly ingredients God had for some reason forgotten to send my way? If I learned to treat women as pieces of meat, become obsessed with the female body, and conquer women physically, would I then find my way into the sphere of noble manhood? If I learned to write love poems, sing love songs, and remember anniversary dates, would I finally solve the riddle of winning a woman's heart?

For years, I attempted to prop up my masculinity with a smoldering gaze, a sultry voice, a mulelike strut, and a tough head nod. But it was like pretending I was a jar full of spicy Tabasco sauce when I was really just an empty glass bottle. There was no substance within. You can shake an empty Tabasco bottle, turn it upside down, and spin it on a table, but no matter how hard you try, if there is no hot sauce inside, you can't even lightly smoke the food the missing ingredients were designed to set on fire.

> A young man will never discover majestic man-ness by trying to compensate for what he lacks.

In the hidden catacombs of my mind, I often wondered if there was a secret to manhood that other men knew about but that I had not been made privy to. *Are there underground kissing schools, sex workshops, tough guy courses,*

23

and cool dance move clinics? And has every other guy been invited but me? I figured maybe my parents filtered my mail and took out all the invitations.

Twenty years of my life were spent in the robust pursuit of gaining this elusive, dangling carrot called *manhood*. But what had I accomplished after two hundred and forty months of burpin' and scratchin', singing with my zipper down, and force-feeding myself Joe Wieder's Weight Gain Powder? My only hope was that somehow, in some way, all my manly pursuits had squeezed at least a bit of fiery sauce into my skinny little Tabasco bottle of masculinity.

I learned the hard way that a young man will never discover majestic man-ness by trying to compensate for what he lacks. He can add steroids, shoulder pads, and war paint to his ensemble, but it will never bring him to the place of complete and polished manhood. A man can be incredible with a woman in the bedroom, a highly trained kisser of female lips, and a heart-melting romantic, but these things will never make him God's gift to women.

The Burp-Olympics

In college, I finally came face-to-face with my complete and utter lack of world-altering man-ness. It happened right smack in the middle of the monthly Stewart Hall Burp-Olympics my sophomore year. I don't even know why I chose to compete in that kind of rigmarole. I mean, unless I had just guzzled a liter of Ramblin Root Beer, I couldn't even produce a quality hiccup. I was reeling from my recent defeat at the hands of Ben "The Burpin' Dude" Barlow when the news flash hit.

I think Ben's burp was actually still going when a Ted Kopell-type character appeared on Ben's tiny little television screen. The words that followed are cemented in my memory.

"This is a special announcement," squawked the poofy-haired news guy. "America is at war!"

Those words lodged in my throat like a cough drop refusing to go down. In slow motion, they repeated over and over again in my head. *Aaaaamerrrrriiiiicccccaaaaa iiiiiisssss aaaaaatttt wwwwaaaaaarrrrrrr.* My masculinity had taken a beating thanks to the practiced excellence of The Burpin' Dude. The reality that I had never been very good at the grosser sides of manhood was all too apparent to me. And now this. America at war.

I staggered across the hall to my dorm room and collapsed on my bed.

Just two hours earlier at dinner, a few of my buddies and I had shared in a lively discussion on this very subject.

"So what do you think *you* would do, Ludy?" asked Ryan with his Texas drawl.

"Uh…," I mumbled, while trying to swallow an oversized chunk of cheesecake, "I don't know. I've never really thought about it."

"If they drafted *me*, I'd head to Canada. There's no way I would fight!" Ryan declared with passion.

"Isn't there something that you can sign up for?" I said,

revealing my absolute ignorance. "You know, if you are like 'conscientious' about the whole war thing?"

A few of the guys laughed at my lack of understanding.

"I heard it's really difficult to do that," interjected Matt, another Burp-Olympics regular. "I think you have to be Amish, or something, to be a conscientious objector."

I was terrified of war. I melted inside when I imagined my name being called out in some large draft boardroom. "Eric Ludy," a booming voice would announce, "you must report to the desert in Saudi Arabia at thirteen hundred hours on Thursday where you will be summarily blown up by a land-mine." I pondered jumping into my roommate Steve's Chevy truck (a.k.a. the Blue Bulldog) and fleeing north to the Canadian border. I even considered migrating east to Lancaster, Pennsylvania, and blending in with the Amish. (Of course, I knew my patchy beard posed a serious obstacle to that option.)

I lay paralyzed on my bed. *America is at war.* My heart raced. I just *knew* I was going to be drafted. I just knew it. I remembered the day, when having just turned eighteen, I was obligated to send in my registration card for the draft. After I placed the card in the mailbox, I walked into the house only to find out that America had just bombed Libya. "I'm gonna die!" I cried out, "They're gonna draft me, and I'm gonna die!"

As I lay there, paralyzed with fear, I was faced with my utter weakness. I lifted weights every day, but this wasn't a weakness as defined by muscles or physical power. This was an internal weakness—a weakness of character. As a man, I wanted to feel confident and strong. I wanted to feel courage and daring stir within my soul. But my Tabasco bottle was empty. I desired something more inside of me to rise up to the challenge, but I didn't find it. No matter how hard I looked that night, *it didn't exist within me*.

It was on that lonely and fearful night, while attempting to prop up my manhood by participating in the Burp-Olympics, that I recognized how far the skill of burping fell short of courage and bravery. It was that night, while pondering a midnight escape to the Canadian border, that I also realized my pursuit of becoming "your everyday normal guy" had shaped me into a spineless wimp, not a brave-hearted warrior. I was on my way to anything but great manhood.

My Introduction to Ultimate Manhood

A few years later I finally got up the guts to enter the field of battle. I'll never forget that heroic day. The year was 1314. On my noble steed, alongside Sir Robert the Bruce, I charged the fields of Bannockburn. My Smurf-blue Scottish war paint made me look strangely like a *Fraggle Rock* character. My plaid dresslike thingee was worn proudly as I raised my fist into the air and cried, "Freedom!!"

I was an inspired man—a radically different man than when I competed in the Burp-Olympics. I waved my sword in the air and challenged King Edward to fight. "You want a piece of me, Eddie boy?"

Yes, this was all in my imagination, but as I read the book

The Scottish Chiefs, I felt my blood stir. I was ready for battle. My hero, William Wallace, had just died a horrible death at the hands of the English, and his example of courage and daring burned within my soul. I wanted to follow him. I wanted to fight for him. I wanted to die alongside him. And as Sir Robert the Bruce called out for all Scottish Patriots to join him in following Sir William Wallace's example, I found myself standing up and shouting, "Count me in!"

On the wall next to my computer I have pinned up a scrap of paper to daily remind me of William Wallace's amazing, self-sacrificial example of the kind of man I want to become. This scrap of paper contains nothing more than a few hastily scrawled, extremely poignant sentences, but I probably read it five times a day. When I do, my melodramatic imagination travels back in time to the moment these captivating lines were written. (They were actually written just a few years ago for the *Braveheart* soundtrack CD insert, but how boring is that?) I picture it as the last gasp of a bloodied Scottish noble. Fresh from the field of battle, sensing his life slipping from him, in a fervent passion for posterity, he scrawls an inspiring message. Scottish bagpipes play soul-stirring tones in the background as he scribbles. His words read:

In the year of our Lord 1314, patriots of Scotland, starving and outnumbered, charged the fields of Bannockburn. They fought like warrior poets. They fought like Scotsmen and won their freedom. Forever.

As a man it's hard for me to read those words sitting down. I feel like I need to raise my fist and howl my best rendition of a guttural battle cry—"Aggghhhhh!" Something deep inside of me is touched by the feistiness of those words, by the raw strength and self-sacrifice portrayed in those few sentences. I find there a vision of manhood that I desperately long to see formed within my life. Those words make me want to learn to fight, to live, to die like a "warrior poet," too!

As young men, we don't often expect to find much in the pages of a dusty old book written in 1820. But what I found in *The Scottish Chiefs* was far more than just great literature; it was a picture of great manhood. So rarely do we see today such an uncommon blend of courage and kindness, of strength and sensitivity, of bravery and servanthood. Sir William Wallace was one of history's most provocative men. His version of manhood was *extraordinary*. It was while riding beside him into battle in the Scottish Highlands, near chapter thirteen, that I first grasped the marvel of a warrior poet. His countenance was calm but intense. His sword was drawn, his cheeks suffused with blood, his lips silently muttering a prayer issued from his heart. He was fearlessness itself in the face of gravest danger. Yet at the same time, Wallace was the embodiment of heartfelt compassion. I marveled over and over to myself, *Who is this man? And how can I get what he has?*

Though far from perfect, Wallace epitomized a kind of

> As young men, sometimes all we need is a picture of what we could become.

manhood that honored and reverenced femininity and would give its life to protect the essence of it; a manhood that feared nothing and viewed courage in the face of pain and death as one of the highest virtues. He exhibited a manhood that valued spiritual pursuit and spiritual sensitiveness; a manhood that esteemed purity of conscience and protection of the poor and weak.

Over the past several years I have charged the fields of Bannockburn many times. Since competing in the now-legendary Burp-Olympics, my concept of manhood has been dramatically altered. I am no longer interested in being just a male with muscles and a mustache (since I can't seem to grow either of them). I now want to be a man with substance. I don't want to be just a boy that plays at manhood, but a warrior poet who actually lives it. As young men, sometimes all we need is a picture of what we *could* become.

Why I Have Written This Book

I want this book to be a vision of what we could become as men. I want the message contained within these pages to be for *you* what *The Scottish Chiefs* was for me. In order to become God's gift to women, we must first become acquainted with a vision of true God-designed masculinity. I want to introduce you to kings and generals, the greatest of warriors, and the most magnificent of poets. I want to acquaint you with a version of strength and confidence that makes mere muscle and a cocky mouth seem like a plastic

Tonka toy next to a monster Chevy truck. I want to showcase a picture of romance so beautiful that you would do anything to be a man worthy of such a pure and celestial gift. I want to walk you into the halls where princes of heaven sit in counsel and where soldiers of Christ prepare their souls for battle. I want this book to enunciate to your heart the very reason that you, as a man, are here on this earth.

I have struggled with the thought of me, skinny Eric Ludy, writing this book. I have long waited for a man from my father's generation to write this book for *me*. I feel, in many ways, that I should be *reading* this book instead of writing it. But while I don't know everything there is to know about manhood, I *do* know the longing that stirs within your soul as a young man. I've felt that same drumbeat within my chest, calling me to something more. Like you, I want a blazing voice from my father's generation to burn a message of hope into my heart and mind. I ache to have a Gandalf-like hero, sagacious in the Spirit of God, thunderously implore me to stand up and be counted as a man. There is something inside me that yearns to have a William Wallace grasp me by the arm and breathe into my ear, "All men die, but few men ever live! Ludy, follow me!"

Yet very few in my father's generation are standing up to show us, with New Testament fire, the path to ultimate manhood. So like young Elihu, the son of Barachel, I *must* stand and speak.[1]

I know that there are great men alive today—men constructed out of heaven's lumber, men made great by the firm hold of Christ upon their souls. But these great men are rare sights, an endangered species. And most of today's older men are too busy to take the time to disciple the next generation. Even if they had the time to train us, they are usually too influenced by the culture's version of manhood to demonstrate true masculine greatness. So we, as young men, stand alone before a daunting mountain that we don't know how to climb.

I was warned before writing this message that it can be hard to sell a book to young men because, as many booksellers have concluded, men don't read. The perception is that, as a generation, we have fallen asleep in a La-Z-Boy with chips spilled in our lap and the remote dangling from our hand. Even more disturbing is the overriding assumption today that men won't change. This seems to be the great unspoken belief of the American Christian world. In my eight years speaking in churches around this country, I've seen the results of this subtle resignation. I've heard it in whisperings from pastors. I've heard it voiced in frustration by women.

Maybe this book won't reach the masses of men out there, but that is not my concern. My concern is *you*. Maybe *you* are the reason I wrote this book. We as young men need just one of our peers to stand up and trust his God completely and without reserve. We need just one who will start climbing the rugged mountain cliffs in the direction of his King. We need just one to hear the call of the wild, to charge the fields of Bannockburn and fight for something that really matters.

I appeal to you, as a young man, to consider that throughout history, it has often been when one young man stood up to be counted that the course of a nation was forever altered.

After thirty-two years, I've only just begun my journey into the endless frontiers of Christ-built man-ness. I have battles ahead that will still shape me. I have tremendous sufferings awaiting me that will purify me and encourage the life of Christ to grow within me. Part of me wishes to wait before writing this book. In twenty years, after I have further wet the steel of my sword in the blood of spiritual combat, after I have ventured a greater distance into this savage life and felt more of its thorns in my feet, after I have intimately savored more of the sweet and transforming grace of my God—would I not be more prepared to speak? The answer, of course, is yes. *But the commission is now.* The time to speak is when the Spirit of God boils the message so hot within you that it *must* come out. The time to write is when God Almighty presses His thumb against your heart and forces the words out like a steaming geyser.

Though I am still young and have many battles ahead, I have personally and intimately experienced the reforming power of the message in this book. To me, this message isn't philosophy; it is real life. My goal is to write about the potential for masculinity, not in theory, but in real-life substance. Some of what I write in this book is still being formed in me. But the truth I write about in these pages is already living within me. I may be young in years and unfit in many ways to deliver such a noble truth. But since my elders seem to be busy fighting other battles, I have taken it upon myself to bring to you the cup that holds the essence of what makes men great. It is up to you to drink.

2

The Brotherhood

The Perverse Education of Modern Males

joined the Brotherhood when I was thirteen. Admittedly, I joined a little later than most. It wasn't like entering a society or social club. Joining the Brotherhood was a rite-of-passage sort of thing. In simplistic terms, when you learn to talk the male talk and walk the male walk, you are allowed into the secret testosterone-filled meetings of the Brotherhood.

Over the years, I learned that the Brotherhood had different levels. I guess you could call them levels of manhood. The more you learned to think, act, and behave according to the Brotherhood's standard of male behavior, the higher rank and title you would receive. I had many sage teachers who groomed me in the art of Brotherhood attitude. Take for instance, a typical Saturday afternoon hanging out with my buddies.

"Hey, Ludy," Milo Richards whispered, "three o'clock—check her out!"

My eyes darted across the Foothills Mall Food Court to my right. Like Vin Diesel on the prowl, I scanned the "plate of food" dressed in a yellow miniskirt, enjoying the visual appetizer. At the virile age of eighteen, "man's real purpose" had become quite obvious to me. Sure, there were those who pondered the vastness of the universe and quoted from ancient books about why we as humans exist. But that kind of stuff was all just hot air! The Brotherhood had convinced me that it was nothing more than a cover, a ridiculous attempt to sanitize God's *real* reason for making man.

"Hey, Richards, don't look now," I excitedly squawked without opening my mouth, "but there's the Häagen-Dazs Beauty!"

"Oooh," Milo lustfully drooled, "come to Papa!"

I guess to some (those aged and balding), man's real purpose seemed too coarse, too debased in nature to acknowledge. But not for me. Don't get me wrong. I would have never dared speak of our real purpose. I was smart enough not to do that. *But I knew our real purpose.* Every guy in the Brotherhood did. In dark corners with hushed voices, when no women were around, we would discuss the secret truths of the male gender. We would chuckle under our breath as we pondered the beauty of the unspoken reality.

There was always a handful of bold guys who spoke of man's real purpose out in the open. They were considered by society to be the perverts, the socially inappropriate, the sex-consumed. But within our male-only dens, we would knight these courageous souls as Heroes of the Brotherhood. What bravery, what daring, what fearlessness! They spoke the "truth" and remained undaunted by the social backlash. We hung pictures of these "heroes" in our minds—the noble Donny Lucero, the illustrious Bobby Gilbert, the fearless Howard Stern—keeping them always before us, so that maybe one day we, too, could be like them.

"Did you hear?" Jimmy Cowles slammed into my locker cackling like a hyena. "The G-Man finally nailed Shawnda Potter last night at Brandon's party! I didn't think *any* guy could get past *her* locked-up knees!" Jimmy and I mused for a couple seconds over Bobby "G-Man" Gilbert's latest conquest, and Jimmy worshipfully muttered, "That guy is some kind of god!"

In the catacombs of my fuzzy eighteen-year-old mind, I had grasped the truth behind man's real purpose on this earth. It was a truth never to be uttered in normal polished society, only to be grunted in the confines of the Brotherhood: *Women were made for the enjoyment and gratification of men.* Excitement surged through me when I thought of it. The all-consuming pursuit of the enjoyment of women seemed so *right*. Everything about it made sense. God created Eve for Adam to "complete" him. Man naturally, even instinctively, longs to experience a woman's body and enjoy her physical beauty. God made us as sexual beings—weren't we actually giving Him praise by adoring His lovely creation?

Sure, it sounded a bit twisted. But it also sounded scrumptiously right. As a Christian young man, I had adopted a less crude version of this "enjoyment" than some of my Brotherhood counterparts. Basically, the Christian version of the Brotherhood stole away most of the fun; it meant enjoying it all from a righteous distance rather than being able to enjoy it up close and personal. Nonetheless, the pursuit of female "enjoyment" was still my subconscious, never-to-be-spoken-aloud purpose for existence.

When I reached my senior year of high school, I received the prestigious Female Preoccupation award from the Brotherhood. It wasn't a big to-do, just the realization that my mind had come under the complete control of this pursuit of enjoyment. "Ludy," the herd of male testosterone beckoned, "you gonna be there for the porn fest tonight at Pete's?" I knew it wasn't the right thing to do, but when the Brotherhood called, I couldn't say no.

At eighteen, I had only just begun in my development as a respected Brotherhood member. I hadn't even received the Proven Conqueror award, like so many of my buddies—that is, I hadn't yet overcome a woman physically. To my shame, the only thing I had gained so far in my pursuit of man-ness was a serious fixation with pornography. Though this addiction was praised within the male-only dens and applauded by the vast congregation of the Brotherhood, mine was still an abysmally low rank on the totem pole of manhood.

"Ludy," the legendary G-Man wrote in my senior year-book, "if you don't use your thingee soon, it's gonna fall off, man. Get some sex this summer, why don't you? You better be a man by the time you reach college."

I didn't allow anyone to read my yearbook that year. I

didn't want anyone to know that I was still a lowly runt in the eyes of the Brotherhood.

This secret society of male testosterone runs deep throughout the caverns of culture, though the secret hand-shake may vary from one group to the next. For example, the "enjoyment" of women is codified differently in religious circles. Christian males are supposed to save sex until marriage, somehow caging the animal instinct in the recesses of our minds until we finally say, "I do!" But many of us within the Christian version of the Brotherhood don't pay much attention to the rules.

"God doesn't care!" Bobby Gilbert pronounced while perusing the new crop of female delicacies at Mountaintop Christian Camp. "All He cares about is that you believe the right things." He lustfully observed a young blonde in a tight pair of shorts and said nonchalantly, "I've had sex with ten different girls, and I still believe Jesus died on the cross. I still go to church, don't I? I'll end up in heaven—so why does it matter?"

Even with Bobby's speeches to inspire me, I was wracked with guilt whenever I let my urges take me "too far." I longed to be one of those unshackled free-wheelers living without the noose of a Christian upbringing. They were at liberty to hunt "feminine meat" as often as they wanted without even a spot of guilt. Yet my Christian upbringing often pricked annoyingly at my conscience, hindering my ability to embrace this Brotherhood pursuit without reserve.

But sometimes, older and wiser church leaders would

come and speak to the Brotherhood, offering pieces of "godly" wisdom that helped to soften my guilt. "It's normal," one local youth leader bellowed. "If you ever hear a man say that he doesn't ponder sex throughout the day, he's outright lying to you. Us guys have 'one thing' on our minds, and that's perfectly fine." Then because he was a Christian youth leader, he made sure to add, "Just don't have sex until you get married."

For a young man enlisted in the Brotherhood, there was no reason to even question the "truth" behind man's real purpose for existence. Even the complaints of abused and sexually handled women were dismissed as overemotional and feministically militant. After all, why question something that felt so good? Why challenge something that was "typical"? Why obstruct something that even most Christian leaders considered "normal" male behavior? Why rock a boat full of the Bobby Gilberts I wanted so desperately to approve of me? Such is the Kilimanjaro-sized rattrap that modern manhood has stepped into.

Women's Opinion of the Brotherhood

"Give me the first word that comes to your mind," I recently asked a young California girl in a very unofficial word-association survey I was taking after one of our speaking events. With a bit of drama, I let the word slowly emerge from my lips. "Guys," I said with a deadly serious face.

"Neanderthal!" She smiled, very much pleased with her quick wit.

Unfortunately, most young women today believe in great manhood as much as they believe Santa Claus can touch his tongue to his belly button. The overriding consensus from today's female population is that modern man-ness, while it is sometimes cute, is only one rung higher than fly larva in its ability to meet a woman's needs. Here's just a sampling of what I'm hearing girls today say about the modern version of guy-hood.

"Simply put," said Kirsti, a vivacious young girl with a knack for swing dancing, "guys are jerks!" (She did add "I don't mean you, Eric!" after she made her pronouncement, but it didn't soften the blow much.)

"I don't know," quipped another college co-ed, "don't guys, like, think about sex once every five seconds?" She furrowed her eyebrows, crinkled her nose, and then, like she had just accepted defeat at the hands of Edward the Longshanks, she added, "I guess guys will always be guys. That's disgusting, but that's the way they are!"

The Brotherhood trains us to let such cutting feminine remarks bounce right off us like bullets off Superman's chest. After all, if girls are really that disgusted with us guys, why do they keep coming back for more?

"Girls like it," Pete confided in me after he slept with Brenda, his first conquest. "They want sex, too. They just *act* like they don't. They try and turn us on with the whole *I'm a virgin* act."

It's funny how guys become experts on women overnight. Take one pair of panties off a woman, and now you have femininity figured out. Pete had a lot of really good insight into the female psyche that Saturday afternoon shooting baskets in the park.

"They complain 'bout us guys always wanting sex," he philosophically expounded, "but they think about it just as much as we do." He finished with a passionate conclusion. "They can't fool me! They want sex as much as we do."

The Brotherhood trains us to justify our actions at all costs. What we do as men, for the sake of becoming men, must above all else be certified as noble behavior. After all, isn't manhood a noble business?

"She wanted it!" the G-Man barked angrily. "I only gave her what she asked for. 'Oh, Bobby! Oh, Bobby!'" he mimicked in disgust. "She was begging for it!" Bobby Gilbert's anger exploded, and he dented the wall with his fist. What to do when you are accused of date rape was not a subject taught in meetings of the Brotherhood. That kind of thing wasn't supposed to happen. Especially since women, as Pete said, wanted it too. But at all costs, Bobby knew he must defend his position—he must defend the right of a man to enjoy the body of a woman. The sanctity of the Brotherhood rested in his alliance with the "truth."

The Brotherhood taught me how to live my life as a man. Unwittingly, I allowed it to tutor me in love, lifestyle, and even Christian doctrine.

It trained Pete Blakely to be, as his ex-girlfriend Brenda titled him, "a Jerk-Interested-in-Only-One-Thing."

It groomed Milo Richards to become, as the Häagen-Dazs

Beauty once exclaimed, "totally and completely disgusting!"

It took the innocent, blue-eyed four-year-old named Bobby Gilbert who made Valentine cards out of pink construction paper for his mom, and shaped him into a cruel and heartless date rapist.

It took me, a passionate five-year-old who sat on my mother's knee and "beweeved" in Jesus Christ and then loved Him so much I took every picture we had of Him in our house to bed with me at night, and transformed me into my very worst nightmare—a weapon against everything sacred, innocent, and true.

The Brotherhood claims that if we only follow its recipe for man-ness, the result will be nothing less than God's gift to women. But actually, the Brotherhood does nothing less than destroy men, destroy innocence, destroy femininity, destroy marriages, destroy families, destroy societies, and destroy the essence of biblical truth.

The Brotherhood has lied!

The Christian Version of the Brotherhood

Have you ever noticed that people sometimes behave differently in church than in everyday life? Guys who never wear a tie on any other day of the week wear a tie to church on Sunday. People who never pray at home, at work, or at school pray with passion and fervor in church. People who would otherwise be embarrassed to be associated with Jesus Christ, staunchly defend His honor within the friendly confines of a church building. There are plenty of reasons to applaud the influence of the modern religious system on the behavior of otherwise reprobate people. But is the modern religious system merely offering "otherwise reprobate people" the opportunity to clean up our act? Or is it giving us the opportunity to act out the role of a lifetime—the part of the "good little Christian"?

Bobby Gilbert would raise his hands when he worshiped God on Sunday morning and Wednesday night and then act like "Jesus who?" the rest of the week. The G-Man spoke respectfully with Mrs. Williams in the Westview Community Church lobby, saying things like, "Yes, Mrs. Williams, classes are going well. How are things in the Williams household?" But the following Friday night he stole her daughter's virginity and bragged about it to the guys on Saturday.

Milo Richards, another of my youth group cronies, could lead an inspiring discussion on "being in this world and not of it" during a Thursday night youth powwow session. But a few nights later he would get mind-numbingly drunk, steal a case of beer from the local 7-Eleven (as if he needed more), and get into a fight with a very large, angry man to top off the evening.

The Brotherhood has lied to us!

The Christian version of the Brotherhood didn't always produce stalkers and vandals; it sometimes produced manhood like mine: spineless, afraid, and insecure enough to avoid doing anything *really* bad—but spineless, afraid, and insecure enough to never do anything *really* good either.

How much of modern Christianity is acting? How often are men just playing a part on Sunday morning, behaving in a way that we know will not draw negative attention our way? How much of our "Christian life" is simply a cover for our *real* life, our *real* focus, and our *real* passion—loyalty to the Brotherhood?

The Christian version of the Brotherhood is a firmly established entity with a long-running tradition of play-acting excellence. From young boys on Bible quiz teams to gray-haired elders serving communion, there is an expectation, a code of behavior, an unspoken creed that most Christian men seem to know but none ever dare utter aloud.

"Look, Eric," a spiritual advisor from my collegiate years once told me, "masturbation and pornography are very normal things for a young Christian man to do. A man, after all, has needs. And if he is desiring to live righteously before God and not have sex prior to marriage, then he must find other ways to vent his sexual energy."

"Ludy," counseled my small group leader when I was twenty-one, "it isn't about the life we live behind closed doors; it's about the life we live as men in front of other people that matters. God knows that we are weak and sinful. He just requests that we try not to showcase our sins for everyone to see."

"Listen, dude!" Bobby Gilbert's words from years before danced in my head when I felt compelled to pick up a sleazy magazine at the gas station. "Don't you think God appreciates the fact that we love His creation so much? If you made something as gorgeous as a woman's body, wouldn't you want your men to enjoy looking at it?"

"Hey, man," the soothing and soft-spoken words of an older and "wiser" Christian man echoed, "God's not concerned about *you* anymore—you're *saved!* Praise the Lord!" He then patted me on the shoulder, squeezed it as if to let me know I was special, then whispered compassionately, "Don't feel guilty about things, man. Christ has covered it all!"

The Brotherhood, even when it slips inside the church walls, can sound so convincing. The Christian version of the Brotherhood is far less vulgar, dresses a lot nicer, and uses a lot of Scripture to validate its opinions.

"Some men get passionate about what they determine to be truth," counseled a religion prof at my Christian college. "Don't ever get emotional over spiritual things. If you ever feel tempted to take Christianity too seriously, then just do what I do and remember Christ asleep in the boat." (Somehow he conveniently *forgot* about Christ clearing out the temple with a whip, calling the Pharisees "whitewashed tombs," and hanging naked on a cross because He loved us so much!)

The Christian version of the Brotherhood promises to make us into a man that can have it all—a clear conscience, a promise of eternity with Christ, a high-paying job, a happy Christian marriage, and all the secret pleasures of the Brotherhood on the side. It builds up the benefits so much that it even tempts normal, everyday Brotherhood members to join the Christian branch. But does the Christian Brotherhood live up to its promises? Well, here is what a fifty-five-year-old ex-Baptist pastor from North Carolina had to say about the matter: "It left me empty of God and waste deep in (bleep)!"

The Brotherhood, Christian or otherwise, is a forceful element in the lives of modern men. For many of us, it defines our thinking, our behavior, our relationships with women, and even how we approach and interact with the God of the Universe. If the Brotherhood said "Eat dirt," most of us would probably eat dirt, because the risk to our manly reputations if we *didn't* eat the dirt seems far greater than the digestive problems that we may incur after we do so. (After all, we can hide the digestive problems.)

The church was built by God in part to introduce us to great man-ness. But instead of being the "Factory for Great Manhood" it once was, the modern-day church has been twisted and warped into a machine that transforms eager and willing men into spineless spiritual wimps.

> If you are not intimately acquainted with Truth, a counterfeit can be quite deceptive.

The ironic thing is that most men don't realize that being spineless spiritual wimps is *not* true manhood. When we are not intimately acquainted with Truth, a counterfeit can be quite deceptive. We as modern men have rarely seen great manhood lived out upon the stage of our culture. And when we have, the glimpse was so short-lived that most of us have explained it away as "odd and unusual."

The Brotherhood has one key objective. Contrary to its

claims, its objective is *not* to make us into great men; it's objective is *to keep us from ever becoming great men*. The Brotherhood will pull out all the stops to keep its members from seeing clearly by cloaking the real source of great manhood and convincing us to buy into a hip and sexy counterfeit version.

All too many of us trust the Brotherhood as our friend. But like treacherous Judas, its kiss on our cheek is not a statement of loyalty, but of betrayal.

The Steel Hammer Theory

Imagine yourself as a steel hammer. Since the time you were first crafted, you have spent your entire life living in a jewelry box, cavorting with rings and necklaces. Your sole purpose has always been to fluff pillows every night for your owner, Martha, before she goes to bed. If this was your reality, why would you ever think that you were made for something different?

But suppose that your jewelry box is left open one day and you see Martha catch her panty hose on a nail protruding from her bed frame. As she shrieks, a longing surges through you—a longing to come to her rescue. "I want to help her. I want to take care of that protruding nail." But reason quickly prevails. "I am only a pillow fluffer," you tell yourself. "I'm unfit to handle a dangerous menace like a protruding nail!"

Every once in a while we young men see a nail protruding from the bed frame of life. When we hear the Marthanian shriek, something inside of us stirs. We look around and notice that all the other "hammers" are resting contentedly in their jewelry boxes, cavorting with all the cute rings and necklaces. So we pass up the opportunity to find our real purpose and finally understand our true design.

But what would it mean for us, as young men, to witness a steel hammer—one just like us—rise up courageously and pound that protruding nail? What might happen to us if we saw a William Wallace, in our modern-day culture, rise up and fight for freedom, protect the weak, preserve the beauty of femininity, and stand up for truth? What would happen to us if another steel hammer jumped into our jewelry box and yelled, "Stand up and be counted as a steel hammer! Follow me—we have nails to pound!"

My steel hammer theory is this: If we young men could see a flesh-and-blood example of what we were meant to become as men, if we could catch an untarnished vision of what we have been crafted for by God—the revelation would unlock the jewelry boxes we are trapped in and set us free to become great "nail pounding" men. Granted, a steel hammer must still *choose* to escape from the jewelry box once it is unlocked. And it is true that he must still *choose* to follow in the footsteps of great "hammers" before him. But once the vision is planted, the steel hammer has the *opportunity* to be something more.

Young men are hungry for a picture of world-altering manhood. We want to know *why* we are here on this earth.

Are we here merely to fluff pillows or is there a higher purpose for us? We need to know how to answer the "call of the wild" that beats like a drum within our chest. We want to solve the longing deep within, to be something *more* in our man-ness than we are today. We are willing to search for it. We are willing to explore this unknown territory. Many are willing to risk everything to find the answer to these questions.

We want to live a life of consequence. We don't want merely to eat, sleep, and burp our way through our time on this planet; we want to inspire others by our choices and actions. But we are a generation that doesn't know how to become that. All we know is what we have been taught—the tainted ways of the Brotherhood. And as a result, protruding nails from the "bed frame of life" are ignored and overlooked by the very hammers that were designed to take care of them. The Brotherhood has convinced us to stay locked within the jewelry box, posing and preening and letting our powerful steel go completely to waste.

We young men don't know *how* we are made, so we are missing our purpose. We young men don't know *why* we were made, so we are missing our man-ness.

The Two Commands of the Manly Soul

Buried deep within the masculine soul are two commands: *protect* and *serve*. God planted these directives within our manly beings in order to lead us in the direction of great manhood. When these basic instincts are nurtured appropriately, they yield the awe-inspiring manhood of the warrior poet— a William Wallace version of manhood. But the Brotherhood has subtly subverted our course.

"Sure, men are to protect and serve," the Brotherhood whispers, "but protect what *really* matters—*your personal image*. Your reputation is king. Make sure you gallantly preserve others' opinion of you. And if you must serve, serve yourself! Ensure *your* rights, honor *your* desires, and above all else, make sure *your* needs are taken care of!"

Such is the condition of even Christian men. When we protect, we protect our Self; when we serve, we serve our Self. We are protecting and serving the *wrong* things. We are lost in the morass of mediocrity, and we don't even realize we are sinking in the slime. We are in a land far from home, having forgotten why we are really here.

"Do not be conformed to this world but be transformed
by the renewal of your mind."[2]
PAUL THE APOSTLE

3

The Battleground

The Sacred Terrain Where
Manhood Is Won or Lost

Young man," Pastor Arbuckle said in his tremulous voice, "beware of the control of Self. If you don't choose the right thing to rule your soul, your Self will rule it for you."

As I was growing up, there were a few renegade voices in my life that spoke a different language than the rest of the Brotherhood. Pastor Arbuckle, for instance. Pastor Arbuckle was an odd man. He didn't comb his hair the way I thought he should. I always wanted to grab a comb, slap on a glob of gel, and fix it. His voice sort of quaked when he spoke, like an opera singer's vibrato. He called me "Brother Eric," which I thought was quite strange. Maybe that's why I didn't listen when he warned me about following the Brotherhood.

After all, Pastor Arbuckle was old-fashioned, antiquated, out of touch with modern-day manhood. And I certainly didn't want my hair ending up looking like his.

Eric Ludy

Then there was Henry, a retired missionary and close family friend. "Eric," he counseled, "if you listen to what the World tells you, it will sound good and will even seem good for a while. But in the end it will inevitably lead you over a cliff." He then looked piercingly into my soul and boomed, "The World will try and convince you that life is all about *you*. That couldn't be further from the truth."

Henry was a grandfatherly sort—nice, but a little on the serious side. He drove an outdated car, wore an outdated hat, and lived in an outdated house. Henry was a great guy, don't get me wrong; but I never looked to him as a teacher in my life. He was distant from the world I lived in. He was far removed from the men I wanted to impress and the girls I wanted to win. What did Henry know about being a guy in today's culture? And so I didn't listen when he warned me not to follow the Brotherhood.

I also received plenty of sage counsel from my dad. But my dad was always...well, my *dad*. For a good portion of my life, I overlooked the fact that I even had a dad; worse, I failed to recognize that I had a *great* one. My dad's influence in my life has been immeasurable. But when I was eighteen, I couldn't see him and I couldn't hear him. One of the Brotherhood's great deceptions is that listening to a godly father leads to wimpy manhood. Maybe that's why I didn't listen when my dad told me to beware of the Brotherhood.

"Son," he gently confided, "God desires to make you into a great man. But you must be willing to listen to a different voice than you are listening to right now."

GOD'S GIFT TO WOMEN

When we protect and serve only our Self, one thing is certain—we will slowly, over time, become deaf to all other voices. The only voice we will hear is the voice that's talking about what's best for *me*. But that voice, left unchecked and unchallenged, will lead us, as good old Henry said, "over a cliff."

The Battle Between Two Voices

When I was eighteen, the voice of Self grew louder than ever before. When I entered college, it grew to a deafening volume: *If you don't look out for your Self, Ludy, who will?*

I had always been a Christian. I could recite passages of Scripture and name the books of the New Testament. I knew the lingo and had memorized all the right things to say. I had mastered the art of fooling people into thinking I was putting Christ first in my life. I had become quite comfortable with my compromised existence.

Ludy, you believe that Jesus died for you, don't you? Why does anything beyond that even matter? my Self reasoned. *You believe in Jesus, so what's wrong with protecting and serving your Self at the same time? If you are doing what the Bible says and trying not to sin, isn't it safe to say that Christ is the King of your life?*

When I prepared to return home for my first Christmas as a collegian, a different Voice began to make itself heard within my heart. Something was knocking on the door of my soul. My Self sensed an intruder and put my soul on red alert status. A battle was imminent. The voice of my Self became almost panicky: *Some people take that God stuff a little too seri-ously. They get all weird about it and never really fit into society. Ludy, don't ever become like that! God doesn't want you to become like that!*

The first wave of the attack came just a few days after Christmas, in the middle of a holiday gathering. I was hold-ing a cup of eggnog in my right hand and a headless gingerbread man in my left, when the first shot was fired. I was taken totally by surprise.

"So, Eric, where is God in your life?" Out of the blue, like a missile raining into an unsuspecting military camp, the question came from an unlikely char-acter named Brad.

Where is God in your life?

For a few uncomfortable seconds, I pre-tended to be chewing on the recently dismembered head of my gingerbread man. But that ruse could only last for so long. "Uh," I finally stuttered, "well…" The right words just weren't forming in my brain.

Brad didn't rescue me from this awkward situation; he just patiently waited for me to respond. Finally, I managed to get something intelligible out.

"I don't know. What exactly do you mean by that?"

"Is God where He should be in your life right now?" Brad gently clarified.

My Self was screaming at me to run, hide, dodge the question, or strategically change the subject. But the new Voice within me began to grow with every passing moment.

I was filled with a strange kind of heat. I found I had an uncanny desire to truthfully answer Brad's soul-searching question.

"No," I confessed, "I know He's not."

To my shame, my face turned red. I found myself attempting to hold back tears. *Tears?* What was this? I didn't *cry*. Brad and I were in the middle of a room full of people laughing and talking. This whole ordeal was getting out of hand.

"Right now God is speaking to you, Eric," Brad explained. "He is jealous for your soul. He wants you as His own."

I had always liked Brad. When I was growing up, Brad was one of the few adults I knew who actually called me by my name. Most of the others referred to my brother and me as simply "the Ludy Boys." So in a strange way, Brad had won my affection and trust early on. As Brad spoke these words of real truth, for once I didn't turn a deaf ear. I really listened.

"Eric, God desires more of you." With that he placed his hand on my shoulder and squeezed it, assuring me, "You must yield to His Voice."

❦

Great manhood is not a difficult recipe involving hundreds of strange ingredients. True world-altering manhood is defined by one very uncomplicated, unpretentious decision. It is certainly not a comfortable decision, but it is a decision that every young man was built to make. If great manhood is to grow and be strengthened, this decision must be made daily, moment by moment, for the rest of that man's life.

The version of manhood that heaven applauds and all hell fears is accessible by all males who live and breathe. However, in every generation of young men, there are only a rare few who find it. These few will deliberately choose to change *what* they will protect and serve with their life. This uncommon band of warrior poets will quit their loyal service to Self and surrender their lives wholly and completely to the protection and service of Another. From out of a generation of young men searching for more, you and I are called to be among these brave few.

∼

I arrived back at college a few weeks following the "Brad incident" a bit disturbed. I was shaken, but I wasn't yet conquered. My Self had been dealt a frightening blow. But Self never surrenders its rulership without a fight.

Come on, Eric. Pull yourself together. Don't fixate on this whole "Where is God in your life?" thing. You don't need to do anything special. You don't need to do anything crazy like change your life. You're doing better than most Christians your age. Just add a little more prayer to your routine. Read the Bible in the morning for a few minutes. That way, God can have His time in your day, while you can live your life.

I had been conditioned by Self not to "respond" to the other Voice stirring within me. My Self warned me not to get crazy, cautioning me to preserve my way of life. But the other Voice was challenging everything my Self wanted to feel, wanted to think, and wanted to justify.

Brad's words haunted me: "Eric, God desires more of you. You must yield to His Voice."

Truth is like an industrial-sized trash compactor. If we get inside it without recognizing it, it will squeeze us until we do. Truth will attack lies. When it strolls into our life, all it needs to do is flex, and the big tough lies that we have always given so much credence to will shrivel up like raisins in a matter of moments.

"God," I prayed one evening before I went to bed, "I know I'm missing something. Please show me what it is."

Manhood is determined in the rugged territory of our masculine soul. In the heart of this untamed region within us is the inner command center of our being. It is in this place that our manhood is either made or defeated. It is from this place that our entire life flows. It is in this command center that our "king" sits to rule. It is in this place that we provide lodging for our dearest "friend."

We are capable of protecting and serving only *one* ruler. Whoever sits as "king" within our command center is that one ruler. Whoever occupies that sacred position is crowned our dearest friend, our greatest love, and our personal biographer of life and manhood.

I remember ripping off the wrapping paper and seeing it for the first time. It was a book. Not even a very attractive book.

They have since designed a much better cover for it, but back then the cover consisted of nothing but the title and a close-up of a man's head. He had a huge pile of black curls billowing every which way and a So-what-do-you-think-about-my-hair? smirk written all over his face. When my sister gave it to me for Christmas that year, she whispered in my ear, "I think you're going to like it."

I didn't plan to read it. It was a sweet gesture by my sister, but convicting books were not high on my priority list. Yet as the months passed, that crazy, funny-looking book stared at me every time I entered my dorm room. It called to me whenever I sat down to study. That piercing yet gentle Voice I had been hearing lately seemed to be attached to this odd-looking book. It seemed to say, *Eric, I have something I would like to say to you through the pages of this book. Please pick it up and read it.*

Finally, I caved. I cautiously picked it up one afternoon, dusted off the pages, and hesitantly started reading. The book, *No Compromise*, introduced me to a musician named Keith Green. Keith had died in a plane crash a few years before, but as I read the book, I felt like he was very much alive. I joined him on a journey through his life, and we became close friends. As I read, a Voice other than the author's began to speak to me. Not audibly, not even in written form. It was that same soft but powerful Voice that had been growing inside me for months. It was a kind Voice, yet penetrating with conviction. Deep inside me, the Voice was calling. It was calling me to follow Keith.

Keith had encountered something that shook his entire being. He had found something that he feared, yet strangely longed for. He had discovered the One who wanted to be his King.

As Keith took steps toward this life-altering reality, I found myself creeping closer as well. As Keith trembled before the holiness, purity, and power of his King, I found myself trembling. And as Keith examined the command center within his manly soul and discovered that Self was on the throne, I, too, was shocked by the realization that Self was the ruling authority in the center of *my* soul. Alongside Keith, I knelt down and prayed. A deeper emotion than I had ever felt churned within my chest.

"Jesus, forgive me!" I whispered in agony. "I have never considered what You deserve. I've only considered what *I* wanted."

As Keith laid prostrate before his King's holiness, he did something that moved me deeply. *He surrendered.* He let go of his life. He removed his loyalty from his Self and placed it with his rightful King. He transferred the ownership rights of his inner command center. I didn't quite know how to follow, but I wanted to.

"Holy Christ Jesus," I emotionally spoke, "I want my life to be Yours. I don't quite know what that will mean for my future, my hopes, or my dreams. But I choose to become wholly Yours today."

~

Majestic man-ness is nearly extinct in our world. The version of Christianity most commonly espoused today is one that refuses to set a knife to the throat of Self and say, "It's time for you to step down—you are no longer in control." The command center within the soul of a man is allowed only *one* ruler. If that ruler is Self, then it cannot also be the true King of the universe. Whom we choose as our ruler defines the substance, the quality, the character, and the eternity of our manhood.

As I said, great manhood is not a difficult recipe; it's made up of one very unpretentious decision. We must bring the center of our soul under the authority of the King of all kings. We must decide to give rulership of our life completely to Christ. We must yield, moment by moment, to our King's command. We must guard the center of our being, keeping it set apart for our Lord alone. We must preserve it from the never-ceasing coup attempts waged by our wily, unrelenting Self. We must rise up and be men. We must become courageous warrior poets, sacrificially protecting and unashamedly serving the King inhabiting the center of our rugged soul.

~

"Dude, I'm concerned about you." Tom said sincerely, an anxious glint in his eye. "I just don't want you to take this whole thing to an extreme."

Tom was a Christian youth worker who really cared

about the direction my life took. During his ministry experience, Tom had seen a number of Christians who, as he termed it, "got weird" in their Christian walks. He identified the cause for this "weirdness" to be a sad case of "overattentiveness" to spiritual matters. Tom felt that Christianity was most serviceable and appealing to society if it were kept in the confines of "reasonableness." The new way I was choosing to live, in Tom's mind, was dangerously close to crossing the line of reasonableness.

"God is delighted to see your zeal, Eric!" Tom encouraged me. "But He wants you just to know that you are safe within His arms. You don't need to do anything more. God doesn't want you to become obsessed with pleasing Him." He paused for effect and then, with one final spiritual gush, he boldly exhorted, "He loves you just as you are!"

When the Brotherhood speaks to young Christian men, it knows not to come directly *against* the Truth—that would be too obvious. It must slightly *twist* the Truth, so that its words still sound right. Yes, Tom was accurate. God did love me just as I was. But He loved me too much to *leave me* as I was. My King wanted me to eradicate any influence of Self over my internal command center. He wanted me to be fully and completely His, not heeding the cost to my Self's desires and wants.

But Tom's sincere exhortation sounded so comfortable, so easy, so right.

Eric! my Self was screaming, you can have us both. It's perfectly reasonable to let your Self be in control and at the same time be a Christian. Even Tom, a Christian leader, agrees! Listen to him!

Gently yet firmly, the new King within my inner command center challenged me to keep walking the path I had recently chosen—*away* from Self, *toward* Christ.

"Jesus," I solemnly prayed as I knelt beside my bed one night in the spring of 1990, "I'm willing to appear a fool to allow You to have my life. Maybe I don't yet know what it will cost me, but Lord, whatever You must do in my life to make me fully Yours—*do it!*"

~

A man is called to protect and serve. The commission is clear. But nowadays, *what* he is supposed to protect and serve is usually quite *unclear*. Many leading Christian voices today offer sweet-sounding alternatives to the recipe for true manhood. They offer models that keep our Self alive, relegating the King of the universe to the unlofty status of a "theoretical king." For as long as Self remains at the center of our inner being, Christ can never be our true King.

Jesus came to earth two thousand years ago for a very specific purpose. Many of us have been taught that He came to forgive us of our sins. That, of course, is true. But it's not the whole story. Jesus also came to deal a *deathblow* to sin. One way to describe sin is this: protecting and serving our Self. Christ came to expose and root out the problem of Self ruling our life. It may not feel good; it may be painful; it may be difficult to accept. But it is the Truth from which great men are made. Our King has freed us from the tyranny of Self. He has freed us from the controlling power of sin. And He has set the stage for a version of world-altering manhood that will rock the nations of this world and make women's dreams come true.

Jesus Christ as the Ruler and Lord of our manly soul—this is the secret of great manhood. Everything else, from whatever Self-made source it springs, is nothing but a counterfeit.

> *"If any man would come after me,*
> *let him deny himself and take up his cross and follow me.*
> *For whoever would save his life will lose it,*
> *and whoever loses his life for my sake will find it.*
> *For what will it profit a man,*
> *if he gains the whole world and forfeits his life?"*[3]
> JESUS CHRIST

> *"No one can serve two masters;*
> *for either he will hate the one and love the other,*
> *or he will be devoted to the one and despise the other."*[4]
> JESUS CHRIST

II

UNEARTHING THE WARRIOR POET

4

The Counterfeit

The Shameless Impersonation of
God's World-Altering Original

hen I grow up, I'm gonna be a fireman, cuz I wanna slide down that cool pole every day!"

"Don't you want to put out fires and rescue helpless victims from burning buildings, too?" my mom asked, trying to encourage me toward nobility.

I looked up at her warily. "Will I still get to slide down the pole?"

At the unsophisticated age of five, we haven't yet learned to say the things that others want to hear. Saying that we want to grow up and be a fireman is completely acceptable, as long as we learn to give the *right* reason for this career choice—to rescue people and put out dangerous fires. We're not supposed to reveal our *real* motive for wanting this noble job—to slide down the pole.

From a young age we search for a testosterone-infused costume to define our manly identity. Each of us as young men must choose how we will clothe our emerging masculinity. Will we become a courageous astronaut? A burly hunter? A passionate singer? A gourmet chef?

"Policemen get to carry a gun," I mused when I was six, "but truck drivers get to sleep in that really neat box-thing behind their seat."

As we grow up, we learn not to be so obvious about the real motives behind the things we're attracted to. We learn to say things like, "If I were a policeman, I could protect society and enforce the law." Admittedly, that sounds a lot more socially polished than, "I wanna shoot people!" We learn to say things like, "If I were a truck driver, I could help society by delivering important packages to busy people," instead of barking out things like, "I could eat all the sugar-cereal I want if I was on the road!"

When I was in the second grade, I didn't realize I shouldn't stare at girls that I thought were beautiful. But for some reason little Michelle Barker always stopped me in my tracks. She was soooo pretty, with her Bambi-like eyelashes and bright blond ringlets. My eyes just kept straying over in her direction.

"Eric," my teacher instructed me privately, "I know that you probably think Michelle is pretty, but it's not polite to stare. It's making Michelle a bit uncomfortable."

As I matured and gained more social polish, I learned how to spy out beauty more covertly. This is quite an art. I learned how to carefully hide my *real* intentions under a masterfully crafted and socially acceptable mask. I learned how to make people feel "more comfortable" while still feeding my appetite.

As a young adult, I mastered this technique.

I remember telling my parents when I was seventeen, "I'm heading off to Mountaintop Christian Camp this summer. I'm thinking it will give me a chance to really focus on God." *Yeah, right!* The *real* reason? A week chock-full of girls, girls, girls!

At eighteen, I told my grandparents, "I'm going to attend a small Christian college. They've got a pretty solid premed program." *Yeah, right!* The *real* reason? A 60/40 ratio of cute girls to what I hoped were ugly, dorky guys.

At nineteen, I confided to my coach, "I'm taking ballet to gain more flexibility for soccer. I really need to work on my flexibility to avoid injury." *Yeah, right!* The *real* reason? A class of thirty athletic girls in tights and only three other guys (who were all coconspirators with me).

At twenty, I told my pastor, "I'm going to Hawaii for missionary training. I hear they have some of the best Bible teaching over there." *Yeah, right!* The *real* reason? A multitude of lovely ladies clad in swimwear.

Even after I had begun my journey in pursuit of Christ, I still knew how to cover up the work of Self.

As young men, we have carefully trained ourselves to hide the rule of Self under a carefully crafted façade. At times, we may even fool *ourselves* into thinking we're noble, servant-hearted, and compassionate. But just underneath the white, sugary frosting is the moldy cake of Self.

⌒

"And what are you supposed to be this Halloween, Eric?"

Miss Johanssen, my first grade teacher, looked me up and down with a concerned grimace.

"I'm a mummy!" I said proudly, moving the toilet paper wrapping away from my mouth. A couple of days earlier, I had listened to the awe-inspiring story of *GI Joe and the Mummy*. From that moment, I knew what I had to be on Halloween. It's still somewhat of a mystery to me how I convinced my mom to let me do it, but when Halloween came, I wrapped myself in toilet paper and scrambled off excitedly to school.

At eight o'clock that morning, I may have looked vaguely similar to a mummy—if you tilted your head and squinted your eyes just right. After the first recess, the Scotch tape holding my ensemble together began to come undone, and I looked more like a boy with a terrible flakey skin disease. By noon, the principal had called my mom, suggesting she bring some clothing for my now half-naked and toilet-paperless body.

⌒

It's bound to happen to all of us wearing a Self-constructed costume. Eventually our "mummy" outfit will unravel. The Scotch tape holding our Self-built image together will lose its grip on the toilet paper. And the next thing we know, we're standing there half-naked and revealed to the world.

As young men, the Brotherhood convinces us to clothe

our man-ness in something that society will applaud and respect, something that women will find irresistibly attractive, or something the church will consider for sainthood. When we are in first grade, we dress in stupid "mummy" costumes; but we later learn to dress our masculine nature in stronger and more courageous-appearing outfits.

We assume the guise of The Soldier or The Hard Worker. The ladies swoon as we arrive on the scene as The Lover or as The Athlete. The Brotherhood cheers as we stand before them as The Adventurer or as The Conqueror. The church gives us a pew of honor when we don the garb of The Sacrificer or The Philosopher.

These are the things that we long to be as we're growing up. We want to be great. Important. Remembered. But if our Self dresses us in these costumes, we are only an imitation— a counterfeit version of the true Soldiers, Hard Workers, Lovers, Athletes, Adventurers, Conquerors, Sacrificers, and Philosophers that God created us to become. *The only true manhood is the version clothed by God Himself.*

The Self-built costumed versions of these manly roles are nothing like the authentic articles. The world sometimes applauds the cheap knockoffs of these masculine identities, but they don't realize how outrageously different they are from the real thing.

We can have all the noble-sounding reasons in the world for wearing these Self-built costumes, but in the end we'll lose our cover—like a toilet paper mummy—and everyone will know it was all a sham designed to protect and serve our Self.

The Real Thing

Leslie and I live in Colorado, so our house has that "rock" finish on the exterior, which lends it a rugged appearance that makes it look like we actually belong in the tough and hardy Rocky Mountain state.

But the "rock" finish isn't really rock at all.

It is *fake* rock, shaped and painted to look just like the real thing.

"It's easier to take care of," explained the builder, "and far less expensive."

We also have a gas fireplace. Don't get me wrong, I really like our gas fireplace. But it's fake. It is designed to make us *feel* like we're experiencing a true, roaring wood fire.

"No, they don't give off the same heat," the builder admitted, "but they're a lot easier to take care of. And just think of all the trees you're saving when you don't buy firewood!"

Like fake rocks and fake fire, modern manhood is an imitation. It's been shaped and painted to appear just like the real thing. It even gives off a token amount of heat to convince those sitting nearby that it's authentic. But in reality, it's just a cheap, easy-to-take-care-of, wanna-be version of what God intended for manhood.

In the world of stone and fireplaces, the difference between the genuine and the fake doesn't pose a serious problem to practical living. But in the world of manhood, the difference between the genuine and the fake is essential. Fake stone and fake fireplaces actually benefit the homeowner—

once you get used to the idea. In the world of manhood, however, only the *true man* is alive and free. The artificial man is imprisoned and dead.

God designed men to be Soldiers of the Cross; Self crafts men to be Soldiers of Self. Both may appear to protect and preserve the innocent and helpless. But only God's original functions as an *outflow* of the Life of his King; Self's counterfeit is only interested in gaining the approval of society. From the outside, you may not be able to distinguish between the original and the counterfeit, but the difference will become all too obvious in time.

> Only the true man is alive and free. The artificial man is imprisoned and dead.

Self's counterfeits have always been more popular than God's originals. When a man lowers taxes, gives aid to the Somalians, builds an impressive megachurch, or gives "all the glory to God" after scoring the winning touchdown, he is crowned a miniature king in the eyes of the adoring public. But God's originals are not motivated by applause or newspaper clippings. They do not live for the approval of men or women. The only opinion they care about is that of their King. As a result, they fight and expend their lives for issues others are only too happy to ignore.

$$\sim$$

A throng of thirty-five thousand cheering, screaming, and whistling fans greeted Christian musician Keith Green the moment he stepped onto the stage. It was a Christian outdoor music festival in the heart of summer, and the pumped-up crowd was ready to be entertained. Keith knew what the crowd wanted, and he knew what he was expected to do. But Keith was listening to another Voice that night.

Keith, his King had whispered to his heart earlier that day, *give them what they* need, *not what they* want.

The audience was there to laugh, to party, and to celebrate in the name of Christ. But Keith knew that his King must always come before what is socially or even religiously correct.

The crowd was whipped into a frenzy and ready to dance the night away, but Keith silenced them with words that cut their souls to the quick. He lowered the boom of Truth. As his King had requested, Keith gave them what they needed that night, and not just what they were screaming for. He challenged them to become true Christians that sing to their Lord out of a transformed life, rather than Christian counterfeits singing about truth but not knowing it in their souls or living it with their lives.

In stunned silence, thirty-five thousand so-called Christians encountered one of God's Christ-built originals. At the end of the evening, Keith asked those who were making a decision to give their lives to Christ to stand up. When almost the entire crowd rose to their feet, Keith thought they must have misunderstood him, so he tried to clarify what he meant.

"I don't mean a rededication. I mean that this is the first time, the *first* time you've ever understood what making Jesus Lord of your life really means."

The crowd remained standing, hands lifted, tears running down their faces, repenting, discovering Jesus Christ in a life-changing way. Because Keith had been willing to obey his King, thousands of lives were eternally changed. He may not have left the stage with an earthly applause that night, but the angelic hosts of heaven were surely on their feet, cheering.[5]

Only God's Christ-built originals say what really needs to be said and do what really needs to be done. Self's counterfeits do what makes them popular and pleasing. Only God's Christ-built originals represent the Life of the King, while Self's counterfeits can only pretend to be alive.

Counterfeit Christian Manhood

"Uh, sir?"

The tall and very serious man looked down at me with an air of condescension.

"Hi, my name is Eric Ludy," I said nervously.

My face was red with awkwardness, and my knees were buckling under the weight of anxiety. I thrust out my hand and he politely took it. He seemed distracted, but I pressed on anyway.

"Your books and your message have greatly impacted me in my walk with Christ," I began.

As I began speaking, his eyes trailed off and seemed to be visually communicating with someone behind me. I stopped speaking. At the age of twenty-two, I was familiar with the dynamics of interpersonal communication.

I paused, seeking to gain his focus before continuing.

He suddenly realized that I had stopped speaking. "Oh yes. You were saying?"

"Uh, sir, I was just saying that I really have been impacted by your books and your message." Again his eyes trailed off, and this time he actually waved to someone behind me and motioned to someone else with his left hand. I stopped once more, humiliated. It was evident that he placed little or no value on my words. I'd wanted to honor him, but it was obvious the desire wasn't mutual.

"Oh, I'm sorry," he said. "If you'll excuse me, I have some rather important engagements on my schedule today."

As today's young Christian men, we are looking for examples of manly greatness. All too often, the moment we think we have seen it shimmering on the horizon is the moment we discover it was nothing more than a desert mirage. Too many of today's Christian leaders *appear* to be Christ-built originals but in reality are only a clever counterfeit.

We thirst for something authentic. We want to find a man who is more than a great author, a great preacher, a great speaker, or a great singer of Truth. We want a man who is a great *liver* of Truth. We want a Yoda-like leader who has trained to be a master of man-ness. We want someone we can observe, follow, and learn from. But sadly, we seem only to encounter half-baked greatness—something that smells wonderful on the outside but is uncooked and useless on the inside.

~

"Marky!"

I looked up, excited, from the thick dusty book I'd been reading. "Did you know that the apostle Peter used to *cry* a lot?"

The topic of "men crying" had become an interesting point of discussion between my brother Mark and me in recent weeks. Did a healthy man express his emotion through tears? Or did tears (as we'd always been told) make a guy look soft and emasculated? Since the question had not yet been resolved, my brother's interest was pricked.

"Does it say *why* he cried a lot?" he asked as he doodled on a piece of paper.

"This is incredible!"

"What?" Marky glanced up from his notepad.

"Listen to this," I said, clearing my throat and moving the big book into a more comfortable position. "The saints didn't know why Peter cried so often. When a rooster would crow, he would cry, and that made sense to them, but at other times he would just break down and weep for no apparent reason." I paused for dramatic effect. "Finally one day, one of the believers got up the nerve to ask Peter why he cried so often. Peter's response was...'Desiderio Domini.'" With that I closed the book and grinned at Marky as if to say, "Isn't that amazing?"

Marky looked at me with measured patience. "Okay. So what in the world does *Desiderio Domini* mean?"

"Get this!" I said. "It means, 'I dearly long to be with my Lord.'"

Now *that,* we both agreed, was a powerful story of an original Christ-ruled man. Peter's tears were not a display of weakness or fear. His tears were a passionate expression of his intense, unquenchable longing to be in the presence of his beloved King.

With only three decades of living under my belt thus far, I have not yet experienced the full and complete vision of everything that awaits God's original Christ-built man.

But I've had glimpses.

There are many historical accounts of great Christ-built men, and these stories have stirred deep within me a hunger to follow them. As a man, it is my dream to authentically cry out, "Desiderio Domini!" I'm not there yet. I have a long way to go to reach such intimacy with my Lord. But it is my goal and my inspiration. Every young man needs a vision of what his relationship with his King can become.

There was a time in my Christian journey when I struggled with constant doubt, discouragement and disillusionment. I wondered if the mediocre Christian manhood I had experienced thus far was all I could ever expect. But then I discovered a passionate relationship with my King that transformed hollow religion into a feast of heavenly intimacy. The very Life of God took complete ownership over my soul and altered every aspect of my existence.

Even at the youthful age of thirty-two, my experience with my King has been beyond what I can describe. I have tasted such joy that at times causes me to think I'll burst in utter ecstasy of spirit. At other times I have sensed a placid calm and complete satisfaction in the power and position of Christ in my soul.

I have the Life of Almighty God within my very frame. Even though I have faced excruciatingly difficult circumstances in my life, His mighty Life within has strengthened and upheld me.

I have the opportunity to spend every waking moment of every day communing with Him, loving what He loves, hating what He hates, and enjoying what He enjoys. I have found a Life that I desperately desire others to experience. I have a roaring fire burning in my heart for God that I must pass on. And I'm convinced that this is only the beginning of what is in store for me with Christ as my King. Desiderio Domini!

"Beware of false prophets,
who come to you in sheep's clothing
but inwardly are ravenous wolves.
You will know them by their fruits."[6]
JESUS CHRIST

5

The Crossing

The Courageous First Step
into Great Masculinity

hat separates Self-serving counterfeits of manhood from God's world-altering, Christ-built originals?

It is a line.

A line blazing with fire.

To walk across this line means extreme pain and discomfort. It means separation from everything previously known and loved. It means invoking the Brotherhood's disdain. It means receiving the stigma of the fool.

There are few who choose to cross this line.

This line has a name. It is called obedience. And it is where a man's manhood is either found or lost. Those who do cross the threshold enter a sacred league. Etched into the sacred doorpost that arches above this fiery threshold is the simple phrase "Choose your king." Those who choose rightly become princes of heaven, warrior poets crafted by the mighty hand of God Himself.

This is more than a decision of mental belief. We can acknowledge the fact that Christ died and rose again on our behalf, yet still choose Self as our king. We can memorize the Bible and answer correctly when asked tough questions of doctrine, yet never cross the threshold of obedience. To know Christ, to believe in Christ, to follow Christ, and to *choose the right King*—we *must* cross the line.

True Christianity is "a cross" and nothing less.

$\sim$

His name was Ignatius, and he crossed the line. Discipled by the apostle John, this man lived a life of utter love and devotion to his rightful King. Deemed a fool, a fanatic, and a plague on society by the Christ-hating culture in which he lived, he didn't cower when threatened with death, beatings, burnings, or being fed to the lions. In fact, those threats seemed only to excite him. The life he lived on this earth wasn't really his life—it was God's. He was completely owned by Another greater than himself, and he wildly and unashamedly adored this mighty King.

One evening, Ignatius was told that because of his passionate and unyielding adoration and service for Christ, he was to be fed to lions the following morning. Hearing the news that he would be ripped limb from limb by sharp and ravenous teeth in just a few hours, a smile creased his face and joy filled his heart. It was time to go home, and he could not contain the pleasure that overcame him. His King was awaiting his arrival with open arms. Ignatius could not have received better news that fateful night. To this man, who chose his King rightly, the lions that would soon destroy his body were deemed his "friends."[7]

⌒

The inner command center at the heart of our manly soul is the battleground of our life. Many of us have been taught that the battleground is our *minds*. But if we try and fight the battle of the mind without first winning daily the battle of our *soul*, we will lose every other battle.

Our mind has power to agree, but it has no power to act. When we choose rightly at the sacred threshold, we crown a new King for our soul. We transfer the authority within the ruling center of our being. We invite a new Life to enter our life. *We ordain a new power to work in our life.*

Right doctrine is important, but right doctrine without the power of the King to live it out is empty religious pabulum. Great men are those who not only understand the Truth, but also allow the power and might of their King to execute Truth in their everyday life.

⌒

His name was Joshua Gianavello, and he crossed the line. He was one of the greatest warrior poets who ever lived and one of the greatest inspirations in my life as a man. Because of his courageous passion for his King, he sacrificed everything dear in his life. Because of his insatiable love for Jesus Christ, he lived a life of unrivaled heroism. His wife and children were stolen from him and brutally tortured and killed. A large bounty was placed on his head, making him a hunted man. Joshua was warned that if he were caught there would be no end to the torments he would suffer. To save himself, all he needed to do was renounce his rightful King.

Though faced with a slow agonizing death, Joshua's response was full of passion, not fear: "There are no torments so terrible, no death so barbarous that I would not choose rather than deny my Savior. Your threats cannot cause me to renounce my faith; they but fortify me in it."[8]

Joshua Gianavello passed the point of reasonableness in his following of Christ. He had chosen his King, and nothing could cause him to preserve his Self again. Such is the resolve of men crafted by the hand of God.

"Hey, Ludy! Do you want to evangelize with us on Bourbon Street tonight?"

"Uh . . ."

I hesitated. A battle with Self raged within my chest. Self desperately wanted to say, "No way!"

Share the gospel in downtown New Orleans amidst the chaos of Mardi Gras? And look like a religious idiot? I had grown up making fun of people who did things like that.

But this new Life of Christ within me was asserting its position of strength. Finally, after a few strained moments of internal struggle, I mumbled, "Okay, I'll try it."

My life had begun to radically change since my days in the Brotherhood. I found myself reevaluating my entire existence. My lifestyle, my education, my friends, my speech, my clothing, my pursuit of girls, even how I spent Friday nights—all of it was now under serious question in the confines of my soul.

I had just begun serving as a missionary in inner city New Orleans when this Bourbon Street episode took place. Evangelizing at all, let alone on a Friday night on Bourbon Street (the hot spot for Mardi Gras madness) was completely unheard of for Eric Ludy, the suburban-born wimp.

As I stood near the van before heading out that evening, I noticed some of my team members loading up two very large oblong pieces of wood into the back end. I hesitated before getting in.

They aren't planning on putting up a cross in the middle of Bourbon Street are they? My Self was horrified: *Run, Eric! Run for your life!*

Downtown New Orleans was overwhelmingly congested on this particular night. Drunken partiers filled the streets. We were forced to park the van several miles away and make the long trek to Bourbon Street on foot. I found myself walking a safe distance from this embarrassing group of Christians. Here we were, ten idiots carrying Bibles, tracts, and pieces of lumber, being gawked at by the smirking onlookers.

Run, Eric! Save your image! Protect your dignity! Secure your reputation as a "normal" human being! My Self was howling to get its power back. It wanted the throne of my life, to regain control over my inner command center. *Trust me, Eric! I am your only hope! Only I can save you from this looming humiliation.*

I was deeply troubled as I realized my shame for Christ and His people. These teammates of mine were the "weird" people that Tom, the well-meaning Christian youth worker, had warned me about. These were Christians that had passed the point of reasonableness in their commitment to their King. They would willingly risk their image, their dignity, and their reputations as "normal" human beings. Even as my Self passionately argued for me to keep my distance, my King wooed me to follow their example. A sacred threshold of fire was set up before me, with the words "Choose your king" etched on the doorpost. I knew I had to make a choice. It was a moment of decision.

When we finally arrived at Bourbon Street, my heart was pounding and my face was red with embarrassment. Three of the guys on my team began to construct the pieces of lumber into a cross. A human sea of chaos and drunkenness swirled around us. I couldn't recall a time when I had been so uncomfortable. All I wanted to do was go home, back to my warm, familiar bed. The huge cross was nearing completion as my teammates struggled to fit the top beam into its place. "Eric," one of them called out above the deafening roar, "could you give us a hand?"

What else could I do but help them? I awkwardly walked their way, still trying to pretend I wasn't really with this odd group of Christians, that I was just a stranger off the street, being polite. Cautiously, I reached up and placed my hand on the top beam, sliding it into place. All the strength seemed to drain from my body.

Everyone's looking at you, Eric! my Self cried out. I quickly backed away into the human pandemonium, distancing myself from the enormous wooden structure that screamed for mocking attention. My heart raced. I had actually *touched* the cross in public—right in the middle of Bourbon Street during the wildest party of the year.

I can't believe you did that! my Self protested. I had touched the fire, and it had burned.

Our team decided to split up and merge with the mob so that they could begin sharing the message of Christ. I remained frozen in place as the multitudes pushed, danced, and brawled all

> I was deeply troubled as I realized my shame for Christ and His people.

around me. I felt like a pebble of sand on a frantic anthill. I was about eight feet away from the cross now. I glanced toward it and instantly found myself mesmerized by what was taking place at the foot of those two pieces of symbolic lumber. The young man holding up the cross was being mocked, spat upon, and shoved. Yet he stood there courageously, seemingly undaunted by the public scorn.

My King was beckoning me to cross the sacred threshold. All I could see was scorching fire, but I heard His powerful Voice beckoning me to surrender to His rule and cross the line of obedience.

"Eric," said the Voice, "choose your king."

In the midst of the tumult, another voice called out to me. "Hey, Ludy!" the young man holding the cross shouted excitedly. "Do you want to hold the cross?"

The sacred threshold standing before me was clear and unmistakable, and it was still flaming with searing fire. These are the moments that make or break us. Trials that test our allegiance can build the stuff of great manhood.

"Eric, choose your king." The inward Voice was strong and insistent.

"Okay!" I finally shouted back to the young man. My trembling legs could hardly carry me the eight long feet to my destination.

Taking a deep breath, I grabbed the splintery cross from the brave young man, wrapping my arm around the base to stabilize it. The moment I embraced that rough wood, I found something that I had never before that moment even known existed. I had crossed that fiery line of decision and in so doing I had unearthed something hidden from my understanding up until that moment. *I discovered the secret of manhood.* I found the empowerment of my King. I realized the matchless joy of giving up *everything* for Him.

Electrifying fulfillment and unshakable confidence washed over me as I stood with my arm wrapped tightly around the cross in the midst of a mob that detested it and everything it stood for.

I stood there for three straight hours, being mocked, spat upon, cussed at, and shoved…and I wished it would never end. I smiled so big and for so long that night that my face

GOD'S GIFT TO WOMEN

hurt for days afterward. Before I had taken hold of that cross, I was just a normal, everyday guy wandering the streets of New Orleans. But once I put my arm around it, there were no longer any misconceptions about my loyalty. I stood in the middle of an ocean of people mocking the symbol of Christ and declared to them all, "I'm with *Him!*"

It was the first time that I had tasted the intimate companionship of my King. It was my very first close encounter with the God who will never leave me or forsake me. It was my first experience with the sheer and transcendent pleasure that courses through your being when you are completely freed from the rule of Self and public opinion and only care what your King thinks. In the midst of a seeming hell, I found heaven on earth. I found the secret that makes men great.

The quest for great man-ness begins right here, with the choosing of our king. Where our quest ends, none of us could possibly fathom. Manhood, under the rulership of Christ, is an endless frontier of discovery and adventure. The crossing of the threshold and the choosing of our King are but the very first steps into this untamed wild.

⤳

God desires us to find completeness in Christ Jesus. He wants us to walk with Him daily, moment by moment, and be transformed into His likeness. But He warns us that we will never find this life unless we really want it. We will never gain it unless we are *prepared* to receive it.

How do we know that we are ready to turn our inner

command center completely over to Christ? Here are some questions we must ask ourselves:

1. Am I ready to have my life invaded by a foreign Power?
2. Am I prepared to have every outpost within my inner terrain taken over?
3. Am I willing to let go of my agenda, my way, and my will, once and for all?

Surrendering the rulership of Self to the Kingship of Christ is the soil in which true men grow. Wouldn't it be so much easier to keep up our spiritual charade and stay in control of our own life? After all, if we give up the controls, what might our King ask of us? Where might He send us? What about our reputation—who's going to protect it? What about our image—who's going to maintain it?

When we step across the threshold of obedience, wreathed in holy flame, we choose to be possessed by a Spirit not our own. That Spirit is the Almighty God of the universe, and He will be Master, Lord, and King over every moment of every day from that time forward.

What is it worth to us to intimately share our existence with the King of Glory? Before taking a step across the fiery threshold of obedience, we must first count the cost.

~

My journey toward personal surrender has been a patchwork process. Through bits and pieces of truth garnered in my college years, I gave my life to my King. There was much more that He desired of me—I just didn't know it yet. I didn't realize that I had only given Him *access* to my house, while He wanted the *ownership papers*. Learning to turn my entire house over to His rule has been a gradual process.

I believe many young Christian men have experienced a similar path. They are eager to serve their King, but haven't heard the trumpet call of Truth above the fog and noise of our culture.

Even after beginning Christian ministry, Self still controlled me in many ways. I had only trimmed the leaves off the thistle in my soul; I had failed to attack the root. I faithfully practiced a version of Christianity that crossed the threshold of obedience periodically, but then pulled back. For a long time, I failed to realize that my King wanted me to enter a sacred *covenant* with Him, remaining in His fiery Presence, enjoying every moment of every day with Him. I learned the hard way that this kind of victory was not something I could accomplish on my own—it only came by allowing His supernatural Life to live *through* me, every moment of every day.

If only someone had spoken this to me—with clarity and conviction—much earlier in my Christian life. How many years of disillusionment and mediocre living might I have been spared? Many Christian men today hesitate to embrace the cross of Christ in public. The Truth cuts, it burns, and all too many of us are afraid to speak it straight. Too many of us balk at the idea that Christ must be given complete access to our soul in order for us to become one of God's originals. We would rather accept a less convicting version of Christianity. But keeping our mouths shut, or even sharing a lesser version, only breeds spiritual impotence and disillusionment.

We may want the benefits that come with great man-ness, *but we must count the cost.* We must ask ourselves if we are ready, as A. W. Tozer says, "to hand over the keys to our soul to the Spirit of the King and say, 'Lord, I don't even have keys to my own house. I come and go as You command.'"[9]

We must ask ourselves some soul-searching questions: Are we sure we want Him to have full and complete control over every aspect of our lives? And, as Tozer suggests, "Are we certain we are willing for our personality to be overtaken by One who will expect instant and ready obedience to His written and Living Word?"[10]

We might want to gain the security of knowing that God is pleased with us, but are we willing to completely relinquish the rulership of our Self to gain it? If we knew what it really meant to die to our Self, what could possibly attract us to such a conclusion?

After all, what's wrong with the version of manhood we have today? Don't people respect us, look up to us, and even like us? Girls might even be attracted to the version of manhood we currently clothe our Self in. Why allow our Self to look like an idiot before the Brotherhood? Why risk friendships? Why make those we love uncomfortable with this new and radical change?

Great manhood stands before us, but right in front of it lies the great test of the manly soul: *Choose your king!*

Our King has already chosen—He has chosen *us*. Now the ball is in *our* court.

Our Self will not let go without a fight. If I could only keep my image, it begs. If I could only maintain my addictions!

But the question that faces us is one that cuts our soul to the quick. It is a gentle probing from the King, asking us, "Will you give Me everything?"

Members of our military earn medals such as the Purple Heart or the Medal of Honor through heroic and sacrificial acts. There are requirements to earn the title "prince of heaven," too. We must lay *everything* down at the feet of our King. The halls of great manhood are entered through no other doorway.

"I have set before you life and death, blessing and curse;
therefore choose life…loving the LORD your God,
obeying his voice, and cleaving to him;
for that means life to you."[11]
MOSES

"Choose this day whom you will serve…
as for me and my house, we will serve the LORD."[12]
JOSHUA

6

The Covenant

The Triumphant Exchange of
Mediocrity for Magnificence

 love to kiss my wife.

A kiss is a tender expression of affection that Leslie and I like to share throughout each day. A kiss to us means, "You are my chosen one." Little kisses on Leslie's cheeks let her know that she is cherished. It's our way of reinforcing our marriage covenant.

Writing Leslie love notes is one of my favorite things to do for her. They don't need to be long to be meaningful. It might be a simple e-mail to her computer saying, "Hey, there's a guy I know who thinks you're really sexy. Do you think you'd be interested in seeing if he is a good kisser over lunch?" Or it could mean dropping a little scrap of paper in her purse that says, "I'm in love with the most beautiful girl on earth!" Whatever the message and whatever the means, it's my way of saying, "You are my chosen one."

I still sing love songs, but now I sing as an expression of

real love. When I sing to Leslie, I use the scratchy super-emotional version of my singing voice that she really likes, and I caress her cheek, kiss her hand, or run my fingers through her hair. It would be really embarrassing for both of us if anyone saw this. But as long as nobody can gawk, it's a romantic, sometimes rather humorous, way for me to tell her, "You are my chosen one." Singing her romantic melodies, in my own odd way, lets her know that she is adored.

But kissing her, writing her love notes, and singing love songs only have meaning to us because of something far more significant that we have done together. Our relationship is what it is because of a life-altering bond that we made together in the winter of 1994.

"I do!" I declared before three hundred witnesses on that tenth of December. "For richer or for poorer, in sickness and in health—I'm your man, Leslie. I am here to protect you and to serve you. You are my chosen one, and therefore, I covenant with you today, till death do us part."

What would all my expressions of love to Leslie really mean if I had never made a commitment to her, if I had never vowed to be her lifelong husband? What would my notes and kisses and songs mean if I didn't prove them to her by the way I live my life?

Covenant is what ties a love relationship together. It's what gives kisses sparkle, love notes meaning, and love songs depth. *A covenant is a binding of two lives, a forging of two destinies for a common purpose.* A covenant, in whatever form it takes, is the most holy, the most sacred, the most celebrated, and the most serious act a human being can make. It defines life, behavior, and all future decisions from the moment "I do" is uttered.

If Leslie and I hadn't formed our marriage covenant, we wouldn't be where we are today, intimately sharing in each other's lives. Sure, we might be able to have a shallow, physical romance, but there would be no authentic, lifelong, always-growing love story between us. For me to access the depths of who Leslie is, and to gain the affectionate intimacy we now share together as a couple, I was required to enter into a sacred covenant with her. I had to make her my "chosen one."

I absolutely love and cherish my marriage covenant with Leslie. But it isn't the most important covenant in my life. In fact, my covenant with Leslie can only work because of a far greater, deeper, and more valuable covenant I forged with the King of all kings.

For years I learned to "cross the threshold" in response to the new rulership of my King within my soul. I spent hours studying my King and learning how He worked, how He thought, and how He felt about things. I sang love songs to Him, letting Him know that I adored Him. But I didn't understand His desire to *enter into covenant* with me. He wanted a fiery bond between us that would sear our lives together as one. He wanted to share my every waking moment, to intimately be part of my existence on this earth. He wanted me to declare, through the forging of a sacred covenant, that "this is my chosen One—I give my life to protect and serve this relationship."

A covenant ceremony always involves an exchange. When I married Leslie, we exchanged rings and vows. She even exchanged her last name and got stuck with Ludy. But we exchanged even more than that. On our wedding day, we gave up our singleness and exchanged it for a shared life. No longer could I just hang out with friends until three in the morning without worry of anybody caring. In this new shared life, someone now cared. I could no longer attempt to win another woman's heart. I had made my choice. I had exchanged the freedom to give my love to anyone for the *commitment* to give my love to *only one* for the rest of my life.

Leslie didn't want just kisses, love notes, and love songs when she married me. As my "chosen one" she wanted a covenant commitment. The same is true with our King. He is eager for us to obey His Truth, write Him love notes, and sing Him love songs. But as our "chosen King," He wants a binding, nonretractable covenant commitment from us. He desires to enter into a holy exchange with us—it's sort of like a marriage exchange on steroids. He wants us to trade our Self-made life for His divine Life within us.

The Preparation for Covenant

"Eric, dear," my mom said, a week before the big day, "make sure you have new underwear for the honeymoon, okay? I've seen your ratty boxer shorts, and let me tell you, honey, those won't be the best introduction to the 'unclothed you.'"

My list was long. To enter into the presence of my new bride on the sacred eve of our wedding day was not something to take lightly. New boxer shorts—check. Haircut—check. New razor for my patchy unwieldy stubble—check. Sexy cologne to mist upon my manly frame—check. Three-hour bath to scrub everything *really* well—check. Cut fingernails and toenails—check. Trim nose hairs—check. One hundred extra push-ups every day the week of the wedding—check. Love letter for her to read when we arrive at the hotel that night—check. Everything else too embarrassing to mention—check, check, check.

"Eric, dear?" my mom whispered to me the morning of the big day. "Please, honey, don't forget to brush your teeth and gargle with some high-powered stuff. I don't want Leslie to think I raised a gorilla."

Check.

Preparing to enter a covenant with a woman is serious business. But how much more seriously should we consider the entering of a covenant with the King of kings?

It goes without saying that Leslie, on the night of our wedding, desired me, as her man, to be hygienically and physically prepared, with all dirt removed, body deodorized, and ratty underwear replaced.

Our God, on the day of our holy covenant with Him, desires us to be spiritually prepared, with all inner dirt removed, all other lovers kicked out, and all other kings booted off the throne.

Removing What Stands in the Way

I am known in my family for my weird and vivid dreams. Sometimes I wake in the morning and stumble out of bed still carrying the feeling of the dream world I just left behind. It's not uncommon that my first words to Leslie in the morning are, "You wouldn't believe what I did last night!" Then I go on to tell her (whether she wants to hear them or not) the wild and heroic dream-adventures of Eric Ludy.

My dreams aren't always noble and heroic. There was one dream I had the other day in which I was standing in a room in nothing but my underwear. I stood frozen, unable to move, sort of like a mannequin. Suddenly, a gaggle of girls came into the room and looked me over, frowning as they carefully scrutinized me. One of the girls pointed at me with a disgusted look on her face and loudly declared to all her friends, "What a *dork!*"

It took some serious counseling from Leslie to get me through that one. "You're not a dork!" Leslie assured me with compassion. "You're just a little strange."

I've had some dreams where I waltz around naked in search of clothes. I've had lots of those terrible ones where I desperately need to go to the bathroom but can't find a toilet anywhere.

But every once in a while I dream a truly significant dream. Eleven years ago I had a dream that greatly impacted me, and I remember it vividly to this day.

There was a long road in front of me, and in the dream, I

knew that the road was freedom, life, and happiness. I wanted to run down it, but I couldn't. In fact, I could hardly move. I looked down at myself and realized I was wearing three things that were holding me hostage, keeping me from moving—prison cuffs holding me back from running down Freedom Road. The first prison cuff was my mouth retainer; the second was a lapel microphone clipped to my shirt; and the third was a pair of soccer kneepads. (This ensemble did not seem odd in the dream.) It's funny how in dreams you can understand strange symbolism, and you somehow know what you are supposed to do. I intrinsically knew I needed to remove these three items, that I would be frozen in place until I finally did.

At the time of this dream, God had been gently awakening me to the fact that He wanted complete control of my life. Even more, He wanted to impart His very Life to me. But I needed to be prepared to receive it. And in my life, there were *three things* I was struggling to let go of. I felt I had to keep a tight grip on these three things if I were to function normally as a man. But these three things had become barriers, hindering my ability to experience the Life of God.

In the dream, I reached into my mouth and removed my retainer. This was symbolic of my Self-image and my ceaseless efforts to be approved by both men and women in terms of my physical appearance. Next, I ripped off my lapel microphone. This was symbolic of my tireless attempts to attract people to my Self through my comedic antics and through my love song serenades. Finally, I removed my soccer kneepads. This was symbolic of my identity as an athlete and my craving for the applause of men.

I was finally able to run, unhindered down the road toward freedom, happiness, and true Life. And when I woke up, I knew it was time to do the same in real life. I needed to remove *everything* that stood in the way of exchanging my life for His.

Inwardly Clean

God is not primarily concerned about our ratty underwear or our foul breath. In God's economy, what really matters to Him is the cleanliness of the inner command center within our manly soul. This internal center is His residence, His chambers within our being, and the place where the covenant will be transacted. It must be shaped into a sacred set-apart place for our King. If our sacred place is broken down, it must be rebuilt. If it's dirty, it must be cleaned. If it's overrun with other rulers, such as Self vying for the throne, it must be radically purged of all potential threats to His complete authority.

I must forewarn you that this process is painful. But though it hurts and injures our Self, it is the doorway into the peace and joy of God. The fire that burns us on this journey is the fire that will set our manhood aflame for the rest of our life on this earth. Very few young men today understand what it means to enter a sacred covenant. God's originals are those who not only understand their covenant with their King, but *protect and serve* their covenant Life with Him above all else.

This is the first practical step in the forging of that new and life-altering allegiance.

Most of us have spent our entire lives in service to Self. The longer Self has occupied our inner command center, the deeper the cleaning must go. This purging process is never easy. But the sooner we begin, the sooner we will discover world-altering manhood unleashed in our life. The super-invigorating feeling that comes with a cleansed soul is an experience that cannot be equaled.

If you are ready to begin this preparation process, I have crafted some detailed material on our website entitled the "Preparation for the Covenant." This material can be found at www.ericandleslie.com/warriorpoet. If you walk through this section prayerfully and obediently, it has the potential to radically alter your life. For the inward cleaning of our being to begin, the light of Truth must be allowed to shine into our soul, revealing the dirt and rebellion nestled within us. If you are able and ready to go through this preparation process, then I would encourage you to do it now, before you continue with this book.

The Covenant Exchange

As I mentioned earlier, a covenant is the binding together of two lives, the forging of two destinies for a common purpose. Our covenant with our King is a binding together of our life with the Life of God. Both of the parties entering the sacred pact give up something to the other, signifying the seriousness and binding nature of the agreement. In a marriage covenant, there is an exchange of rings, vows, possessions, even of last names. But in this covenant there is an exchange of *life*.

Two thousand years ago Jesus Christ died a harrowing and horrible death, giving up His life for us. After being raised from the dead and ascending into heaven, He made *His very Life* available to us. The holy, all-loving, all-powerful, all-mighty, perfectly peaceful and joyful Life of God is waiting to be ours. It is a priceless gift that comes with only one condition: His Life can only be had in exchange for our own.

> His Life can only be had in exchange for our own.

Jesus Christ yearns for soldiers of the Cross to rise up. He's longing to have warrior poets trek this earth again, men with the very Life of God beating within their chests. But true warrior poets are shaped in the *flame of surrender*.

To enter into this sacred bond with our King, we must come humbly to the covenant altar and say "I do" to these four questions:

1. Do I choose to forgo my reputation, my image, and forget what others may think of me? Do I choose to make the opinion of my King the *only* opinion that matters? Do I choose to lose my identity in Jesus Christ and risk appearing the way He appears to this world—as a fool or a fanatic?

2. Do I choose to make my life, my abilities, and my resources available to my King, for Him to use in what-

ever manner He may see fit? Do I choose to make the minutes and hours within my day completely and unreservedly available to my King, for Him to define and structure in whatever manner that pleases Him? Do I choose to make my physical body a tool in the hand of my King—allowing Him to send suffering or pain or pleasure, according to His good plan?

3. Do I determine to make the pursuit, service, protection, and enjoyment of the Life of my King my primary focus for each and every day for the rest of my life? Do I choose to remove anything that would stand in the way of cultivating that Life? Do I choose to give up even "good" things if they hinder my love relationship with my Lord or hinder others from finding His Life?

4. Whether living in plenty or in want, in sickness or in health, do I choose to faithfully serve and love my King? And do I choose to trust Him no matter what difficulties I may face or hardships He may choose to bring my way?

The covenant with our King is a solemn vow. It's a covenant that reaches into eternity. We remember it every time we take communion (the Lord's Supper). By taking the bread and the wine, we are saying, "I remember, cherish, and praise You, Jesus Christ, for the Life You have given me. And today I also remember that I am Yours, completely and unreservedly. My body is for You to break, and my blood is for You to pour out as You see fit. I am Your man, and this is Your Life!"

God's gift to women is formed right here, in the inner

command center of the manly soul. A man with the holy fire of God burning in his chest is capable of setting a woman's heart on fire for a lifetime.

The Covenant Life

Throughout the rest of this book, I will refer back to this covenant Life that we share with our King. It is this Life that begins our intimate adventures with Jesus Christ, and it is this Life we will share throughout all eternity. It is a life of daily moment-by-moment leaning on our King's strong and powerful chest. It is a life of adoration and enjoyment, delighting each and every minute in His constancy, His faithfulness, His love, and His heroic strength.

This covenant Life is what the apostle Paul describes as "the mystery hidden for ages and generations."[13] It is the great gift of the Cross, the promise of victory, and the life-altering substance at the foundation of Christ-built manhood. Discovering the covenant Life is discovering the lost greatness of masculinity.

The covenant Life is Jesus Christ ruling my soul, sharing His very Life with me, revealing an ever-increasing amount of His greatness to me as each day passes. The covenant Life is the great treasure of God's very Life shared intimately with my own. It's my Self shrinking from its rulership position to allow the mighty God of the universe His rightful place as the master of my existence. Rather than clinging tightly to my own wants, desires, and dreams, I must now daily relinquish them to my King, declaring, "*Your* will, not mine, be done." Rather than yielding to the inward whisper of my Self, I must now yield daily to the still, small Voice of my King, gently guiding and directing every step of my life. Rather than using my own strength to overcome sinful habits, I must now lean on the unshakable strength of my King working in and through me to lead me to victory.

Entering the covenant Life is not a one-time decision. It is a daily, moment-by-moment, ever-deepening relationship with the King of my soul.

> *"I have been crucified with Christ;*
> *it is no longer I who live, but Christ who lives in me."*[14]
> PAUL THE APOSTLE

> *"Do you not know that your body is a temple*
> *of the Holy Spirit within you, which you have from God?*
> *You are not your own; you were bought with a price."*[15]
> PAUL THE APOSTLE

7

The Complete Man

The Prince Every Woman Dreams Of

ric, a woman is the proving ground for a man."
It was halftime during the big Colorado-
Nebraska football game. My dad was offering
counsel over a fresh bag of Tostitos and the Ludy favorite,
cream cheese-and-salsa dip.

I was twenty-two years old and valued the opportunity
for a little serious guy talk with my dad. But where was he
taking the conversation? One minute we were chatting about
Bill McCartney, coach of the Colorado Buffalos; the next we
were talking about George Washington and his tremendous
example of manhood. Then suddenly my dad spurts out that
"woman is a proving ground" statement. What was he talking
about?

I crunched into another chip, figuring he had strayed
from our original point. Even so, I found myself interested in
this new line of thought.

"The way a man treats a woman," he explained, "is a

reflection of his relationship with God. That's why I say a woman is the proving ground for a man. You can determine a man's quality by watching him with a woman."

~

Young men have a weakness. *Girls!* The Brotherhood (a.k.a. Satan), of course, understands this very well. Only our covenant Life with the King can help us thwart this masculine propensity to serve our desires and fan our lusts into flame. The Brotherhood has twisted our thinking in this area, and it's about time we Christ-built men got it straight again.

Women are men's greatest weakness; but they are also our proving ground for greatness. If we can implement our covenant Life as we relate to femininity, we will have successfully trekked over one of the most dangerous mountain passes a man must venture.

Please understand, although this book is largely about how we, as men, relate to women, I am by no means endorsing the idea that a man is not complete without a woman at his side. I am, however, a firm believer that a man is not complete without the covenant Life of his King beating within his chest. And a crucial extension of that covenant Life, for a high percentage of us, is learning to faithfully protect and serve femininity.

Christ-built men have a major advantage over Self's counterfeits in the romance department. Self-made men, no matter how they try to produce intimacy, love, and tenderness, in romantic relationships, can only achieve a counterfeit result—something that ends up being similar in appearance but vastly different in nature. Christ-built men have the opportunity to understand and experience intimacy, love, and tenderness on a level that Hollywood can never touch.

The Quiz

Do guys today know what it takes to win a young woman's heart? Leslie and I posed this question recently to a group of college-age females. Almost immediately, a redheaded girl with boysenberry nail polish retorted, "They have no clue!" A blue-eyed sorority sister muttered sarcastically, "Yeah, right!"

We took a similar question to a group of young males. "What does it take to win a young woman's heart?" We started with Chad, a WWF fanatic with a nose ring and perfect attendance at his Gen X church. When he found out that his reply might end up in a book, he took his time. After a few weighty and ponderous moments, he finally stuttered, "Uhhhh, I dunno." Suddenly scratching his arm real hard—like he'd had a sudden attack of the chicken pox—he added, "I guess they like things like flowers and stuff."

Ellis, a super-tall, super-thin, Afro-sporting drummer, didn't take the same amount of time before pronouncing his opinion on the matter: "I think girls like a little attitude. You know, a cocky kinda guy."

A husky nineteen-year-old, Bubba, offered the most interesting response. Bubba sported a shaved head and baggy jeans and gnawed on a piece of gum (Hubba Bubba?) as though his life depended on it. "Girls don't have a clue what they want, man!" he exclaimed with a noticeable hint of frustration. "They are *totally* confused!"

As a man, I can easily climb into Bubba's world. I have felt Bubba's pain.

Many a well-meaning man through the centuries has convinced himself that "women are totally confused." But the truth is, *women really do know what they want.* Most girls grow up dreaming of knights in shining armor and fairy tale romances. But as these girls get older, they are faced with a version of manhood so far beneath their ideal that they begin to think that such dreams are unrealistic. Since today's young women see only male mediocrity everywhere they look, they learn to settle for today's burpin'-and-scratchin' version of manhood and deny the fact that they ever wanted something more.

So why do modern women come across as so confused in their desires?

Because their fairy tale dreams never truly die. Thus we find the "confused" modern woman—one moment desiring men to be warrior poets while in the next moment denying the fact that she ever expected men to be anything other than burpers and scratchers.

The longings of a woman's heart will likely remain unspoken unless a guy makes a focused effort to really understand her dreams and desires. If a man never understands a woman's heart, he will never know how to win it, protect it, and cherish it.

Oh yes, women know what they want. But today's guys, like Chad, Ellis, and Bubba, aren't even close to figuring it out. In fact, we men have been taught that, no matter how hard we try, we will *never* figure women out.

It's a lie! It is true that authentic, God-designed femininity should always hold a certain mystery for us men. Even so, we *can,* if trained, learn how to understand a woman and nurture her heart. And this is crucial to our success as men, whether we ever get married or not.

As my dad said to me so many years ago over a bag of Tostitos, you really can't talk about manhood without bringing womanhood into the discussion. The Brotherhood trains us, as young men, to study the "female shopper," learn her likes and dislikes, and discover her interests and wants so as to conquer her emotionally and/or sexually. Indeed, God *did* intend us to study and understand our feminine counterparts, but not for the reason the Brotherhood has offered.

Encrypted within the amazing design of authentic femininity is a golden key for men. It's a key that can unlock for us the mysteries of relational success with family, friends, a future bride, and most importantly, with our King.

Stuck Somewhere in Kansas

It goes without saying that guys don't like to ask for directions. I remember five of us piling into my college roommate's tiny little Toyota and heading off to Nebraska. "Turn here!" I yelled from my squished position in the backseat. "This is the interstate that takes us there!" My confidence and evident road knowledge won me great points with the other four "dudes." We guys really respect things like confidence and directional savvy.

That is, they *were* really impressed with me—until my directions landed us in the middle of Kansas.

In response to the first naysayer remarking, "Hey, Ludy! Why are we in Kansas?" I politely responded, "Don't you know that you have to go through the corner of Kansas to get to Nebraska from Colorado?"

That shut him up for a while. Since we didn't have a map in the car, no one could really argue with me. But seventy-five minutes later, while still in Kansas, the naysayer gained more confidence. "Hey, Ludy! Just how big *is* this corner of Kansas?" My pride was at stake. I had absolutely no idea where we were, and this loudmouth friend of mine was exposing that fact.

When we understand women, we understand a huge element of manhood.

After another two hours venturing into the heart of Kansas, I stuck a fork in my pride and mumbled something very unmanly from the backseat. "Uh…guys…maybe we should stop and pick up a map."

We men have adopted the concept that "not asking for directions" is the essence of manliness, when it is actually the essence of stupidity. Modern-day manhood is lost somewhere in Kansas, and we're too proud to let anyone know it. We think that if we just keep heading east on I-70, we'll eventually arrive at the city of Great Manhood. We have a vague idea, from what other guys have told us, of how to get there; but the farther we go, the more it becomes obvious (to everyone except us) that we are a lot closer to Jerksville than we are to anywhere else.

We imagine we'll do just fine starting out on a road trip without compass, map, or directions, and in the same way, we tell ourselves that we don't need to listen to the women in our lives. *Why ask a woman what she thinks?* we reason. *Men have all the answers, and women just confuse the issues!* As a result, we find ourselves in a dumpy little Toyota stuck in the middle of Kansas with more hope of meeting Dorothy and the Wizard than we have of reaching the city of Great Manhood.

Two Missing Ingredients

My dad said it well. "Eric, become a student of your wife. And then you'll know what it means to be a man."

When we, as men, understand women, we will understand a huge element of what manhood was meant to be. God's original Christ-built man is a *helper* and *advocate* of radiant, Christ-centered womanhood.

Covenant-controlled manhood, polished and perfected by the Spirit of God, is marked by two specific qualities. These two qualities, when developed properly, transform the world around a man—and magnetically attract a woman's heart:

1. **We must learn to be a warrior.** More than just a defender of justice and champion for the weak, a true warrior is a heroic protector of the covenant Life within his being. As an <u>outflow of that covenant Life</u>, a warrior is trained to protect that which is sacred and innocent within a woman.

2. **We must learn to be a poet.** More than a bearer of roses, rings, and rhymes, a true poet cultivates an intimacy with Christ; and <u>as an outflow of that intimacy</u>, he is trained to understand and appreciate the intimate sanctuary of a woman's heart.

Both of these qualities work together to produce a version of manhood that can truly be God's gift to women.

A Guy Named Chuck

Let's take a peek into the life of a young man named Chuck. According to most definitions, Chuck is not just your average burpin'-and-scratchin' male with high testosterone levels. In fact, he represents a deluxe version of modern-day manhood and is a candidate for many a young girl's "most eligible bachelor" list. Take a look at his résumé.

Chuck is a leader in a student outreach ministry at his college. He's a "save sex till marriage" kind of guy. He's even a believer in good hygiene and the daily use of deodorant. And get this—the girls in his campus Bible study swear that he has Brad Pitt's boyishly charming smile and Tom Cruise's smoldering gaze. "When he looks at me, I just melt," giggling girls have been overheard saying. For most girls, that would be enough to sell them on Chuck as this generation's equivalent to William Wallace.

Chuck, however, has a few significant problems.

To the rest of us, he comes across as "so much better than the average." Just beneath the surface, however, there is little difference between the "burpers and scratchers" and Chuck. Although he can quote Scripture better than your average dude with a college degree, Chuck still learned the basics of manhood from the same school as most of the guys in his generation—the Brotherhood.

Like other males his age, Chuck is a firm adherent to the one-thing-on-the-mind version of manhood and has practiced it with great dexterity for years. Pornography has been a shameful vice of his for a decade now, and it has helped to train him in the idea that the female body is meant solely for his personal Self-pleasure. Without intending to, Chuck has allowed himself to be educated in the school of counterfeit Christian manhood. And he would probably even be shocked to realize that he subconsciously thinks femininity is important only so far as it brings him enjoyment.

Chuck may be a step above the typical guy today, but he is a sad substitute for God's original Christ-ruled man. Wearing a WWJD T-shirt doesn't change what's in his heart. His training in manhood has left him fully equipped to enjoy the opposite sex, but outrageously *ill*-equipped to have the opposite sex enjoy him. He has trained himself to appreciate the outer shell of the female body, but he is empty-pocketed and poorly groomed to understand and serve the inner needs of a woman.

Chuck the Great Hunter

When Chuck first encounters Sarah at his weekly campus outreach meeting, he plays the part of the good Christian man. "Hi, my name's Chuck." He enthusiastically stretches out his arm to offer a firm but friendly handshake and adds, "Is this your first time here at the Spirit Zone?"

Sarah is quick to notice Chuck's boyish smile. Her knees weaken just a bit. "Uh," she stutters, "yeah, I just transferred in from ACC."

"Well, let me show you around." With a charming twinkle in his eye, Chuck takes her coat from her and begins the tour.

Even though later that night Chuck will describe Sarah to his buddy Dexter as "one super-sexy piece of Christian (rear end)," he dares not expose his Brotherhood motives while in Sarah's presence. While he is with her, he says things like "Yeah, I'm thinking of going into ministry" and "I'm considering taking up guitar—they need a new worship leader here at the Spirit Zone on Tuesday nights." He even tries the line I always liked to use while under the hypnotic control of the Brotherhood: "I just really have a heart for the orphans over in Romania."

Great hunters study the behavior patterns of their prey.

To kill an elk, for instance, demands great patience, a sharp mind, and an understanding of this majestic creature. If you ask a hunter why he studies the elk, he will tell you it is not so that he can *help* the elk, but so that he can *conquer* it. His interest in the elk is the thrill of conquest. He has no interest in feeding it, nurturing it, or coddling its young. Unfortunately, young men like Chuck have been taught to apply this same hunter's mentality to their pursuit of women. We attempt to understand the female of our species, not so we can take care of her or protect her from harm, but so we can conquer her emotionally and/or sexually, and in so doing, boost our status on the totem pole of manhood.

Chuck has been trained to pursue the complete conquest of the lovely Sarah Billington. Sure, he's a save-sex-till-marriage dude, but most of that is just for show. The act is necessary to make her trust him and to lure her into his snare. A good girl like Sarah would never fall for him if he ever divulged his secret intent.

Chuck really does wish that he could wait until marriage to have sex with Sarah. It would make God happy and probably be a far more respectable thing. But as he shared with Dexter, "this Christian save-sex-till-marriage thing really stinks!" Forget the fact that Sarah wants to save herself until marriage. Forget the fact that he's a leader of a campus ministry and, therefore, an example of Christ to a secular campus. The Brotherhood makes it quite clear: Play at your Christianity, but live out your Brotherhood dreams.

Not long into their dating relationship, Sarah discovers

the truth about Chuck. He wasn't really interested in protecting and serving her, warrior poet-style. He was interested in conquering her, Brotherhood-style. Chuck could only cover his counterfeit version of manhood so long. Two months later, after a pregnancy test proves positive, Chuck and Sarah walk down the aisle to share life together as one.

When Chuck Gets Married

If you take our young man, Chuck, and train him to have "one thing" on his mind, train him to place the interests and needs of women beneath his own, and train him to be insensitive to, or even unaware of, the unique demands of femininity—then what exactly happens to Chuck after he utters the words "I do"?

Does Chuck, the newly married man, rise to the challenge that marriage offers? Does he change his ways and learn to be a great man? Or does he entrench himself even deeper in the ways of Brotherhood-built manhood? Is marriage today a cocoon for young men to be transformed into great men, or is it a place where stubborn mules just grow more stubborn?

In case you haven't noticed, we're not hearing many married men today stand up and say, "Wow, I just love marriage!" We seem to only hear "stubborn mulelike" complaints. One of the top complaints of married men today—and this includes Christian men—is that they are not fulfilled sexually by their marriage partners. Simply put, the cry from men today is "We want more!"

I asked some young married men just what they wanted "more" of in their marriages. I put it to them like this: If you could choose between having either more relational intimacy with your wife or more sexual passion in the bedroom, which would you choose?

"What do *you* think?" a twenty-seven-year-old husband chuckled. He'd been married four years—long enough to know what he really wanted. As a guy, I instinctively knew what he meant by that answer. He was looking at me as a fellow member of the Brotherhood, saying, "You know, Eric, that we men are only interested in one thing!"

A thirty-something groom that I queried only laughed as if to say, "Do you even need to ask that question?" I sensed a *What type of guy wants intimacy?* sentiment that seemed to be shared by every guy I polled. One witty respondent added a little diversity, saying, "Do you want the *right* answer or the *real* answer?"

Sadly, the majority of modern-day guys are fairly predictable when it comes to our interaction with women.

Lost in Kansas Again

Most guys today can tell you what they want.

"I want a steak, medium-rare, and a baked potato with sour cream on the side."

"I want a lot of money, a black Hummer with mud on the tires, and a pit bull to protect all my stuff!"

"I want a bag of Doritos, a six pack, and seventy thousand

screaming football fans to party with via my big-screen TV."

Guys know what they want in the female department, too. The universal cry seems to be "I want sex!"

Even writing this, I am profoundly ashamed of what we, as guys, have become. Most of us are proud to be this disgustingly predictable. <u>Our problem doesn't lie in the fact that we are uncertain in our wants, it's that our wants are crippling us.</u>

Just like an arrow is fashioned to hit a target, young men are meant to hit a target with their lives—to be shaped into Christ-built men. This culture has trained us instead to shoot our arrows, not at the target of ultimate manhood, but haphazardly up into the air. Then like stooges we can't figure out why those same arrows rain like meteors right back down upon our lives, wounding and maiming us.

We guys may be in touch with our wants, but our wants are all wrong. We assume that if we follow our programmed desires, if we follow the map of the Brotherhood, we will end up in the city of Great Manhood. But by following these flawed maps, we are instead ending up on the wrong side of the manhood continent—in Jerksville.

> We seek the city of Great Manhood, but instead we are ending up in Jerksville.

We need to alter our wants, retool our approach to finding true manhood, and use a "new" map on our journey. If we allowed every aspect of our manhood to <u>flow out of our covenant Life with our King,</u> we would end up with far more in our lives as men than we ever dreamed or imagined.

Chuck Revisited

Let's catch up again with Chuck. Like the huge majority of men today, Chuck finds himself somewhere in the middle of Kansas. His map is either nonexistent or just plain wrong. He isn't anywhere near the welcome sign to the city of Great Manhood. Chuck, even as a Christian man with Scripture stored away in his brain, isn't doing so hot at this marriage thing. And like multitudes of married men today, he has a complaint. In fact, he is faithful to bring this complaint to Sarah's attention at least twenty times a week. The long and short of it is that he wants more sex in his marriage. In fact, in recent days he would be happy with just a *little* sex in his marriage. As far as Chuck is concerned, "This marriage ain't going nowhere unless we add in some sex!"

Over the first five years of their marriage, Sarah, his patient and loving wife, has repeatedly pled with Chuck, "I just need more time with you. I need you to listen to me. I need for you to do sweet things for me."

Chuck scoffs at such suggestions.

According to his makeshift Brotherhood map, real men don't do things like that. According to his map, his wife's body is for his enjoyment, and his wife should submit to his wants and needs for sexual passion. The farther Chuck goes in the wrong direction while following his map, the more mystified and frustrated he becomes. His wife becomes increasingly resistant to his whining overtures. He has wants, but she doesn't seem to care.

The very thought of sexual closeness with this jerk is becoming, with each passing day, more and more repulsive to Sarah. In Chuck's mind, however, it must be his wife's fault. His wife should accept him the way he is because, according to his map, he is a model of true manhood.

I want to grab him—and the countless other "Chucks" out there—by the scruff of the neck and say, "*Listen* to your wife! If you would simply listen, you would realize that she holds a secret key of success for you!" Even after thirty years of marriage, a man like Chuck can miss something that is so painfully obvious. If only Chuck had simply responded to his wife when she said, "Baby, I just need more time with you." If only Chuck had listened when she pleaded, "Chuckie, I need you to listen to me." If only he had taken her seriously when she whispered, "Chuck-ee-poo, I need you to do sweet things for me every now and then." Through all those weeks and months, his wife was trying to hand him a map to a buried treasure that would have made Long John Silver envious. His wife was giving him the very ingredients that make for sexual passion in a marriage. She was showing him how to find the very thing he was searching for.

In a few critical man-making areas, women, for some reason, have been given an ability to see things that we men can't. They see the underground caves that lead to the buried treasure, whereas we men see only the buried treasure and are clueless about how to access it. We whine for the treasure but never find it, because we didn't allow the "map-bearers" to tell us *how to* find it.

Of course it's true that women, like men, are only human. They, too, have their faults and imperfections. But because of the way God designed them, women intuitively know that relational intimacy should be the goal for a healthy marriage. Relational intimacy between a man and a wife will *naturally* bear the fruit of increased sexual passion. Married men would find amazing satisfaction if they could first realize that their map has for years been defining the wrong thing as the actual treasure. Men complain about the lack of sparkle in the bedroom, but they fail to realize that understanding their wives is the key to finding it. Married boys are shaped into married men when they finally recognize that the buried treasure isn't the act of sex—the buried treasure is knowing, loving, and sharing the most intimate aspects of life with that woman sleeping next to them every night.

Worse, as modern-day "Chucks," this cluelessness is not just affecting our marriages, but it is also hindering our personal relationship with Jesus Christ. Just as relational intimacy is the essence of what makes a marriage great, it's also what makes a Christ-built man great. Christian men desperately need a new map, because our current one leads not only to mulelike married men, but also mulelike Christian men. We long for the treasures of Christ's kingdom, wondering why God won't entrust us with more, and all the while we neglect to explore the underground caves that would actually lead us to that precious store. We men think the buried treasure is something that we *receive* from Christ, when in actuality, just like in marriage, the true treasure is knowing, loving, and sharing the most intimate aspects of life with the Lover of our soul. We don't understand intimacy with women, let alone the most important form of intimacy—intimacy with our King.

Let's turn our little Toyota around and start heading in the right direction. Here are six things that we can begin to start doing right now:

1. **Enter into a covenant Life with our King.** We may desire to be great men, exhibiting the nature and character of Christ, but we will only remain a counterfeit version of manhood until we make the great exchange—our life for His. A warrior poet must first of all be in close relationship with his King.

2. **Study womanhood.** Most of us are fairly knowledgeable about the outside of a woman. But we need to start focusing on the *inside*. We need to get acquainted with how femininity works, how it feels, how it dreams, and even how it thinks. For the past few years, I have kept a journal that I call "Studying Womanhood." In it I write my observations about how Leslie thinks and feels. My desire is to become the ultimate protector and servant of my wife. To do that I have to know *how* she needs me to protect her and *how* she needs me to serve her. If we young men want to be strong in marriage, we must become students of femininity. Start your journal today.

3. **Journal your journey of manhood.** If you will implement the message of this book, you can experience a

massive overhaul of your entire life. Don't lose a bit of it. Write it all down. Not only will it be super encouraging to look back to see your growth, but it will be an invaluable tool to assist you in helping other young men along the journey. I have kept a personal journal since February 1990. If my house was on fire, the first thing I would rush inside to look for, after my family members, would be my journals. They chronicle both my covenant Life with Christ and my covenant life with Leslie. Writing in a journal has not only groomed me as a writer but has also provided me material that I use in writing books. Capture your journey. You will not regret it.

4. **Write love letters to your future spouse**. You don't have to be married to protect and serve your wife. Even if you don't know who she is, you can begin to practice being a warrior poet, protecting and serving her interests today. Your mission is to protect for her the purity of your mind, your heart, and your body. So protect and serve *her* now by setting your life aside as a sacred monument of loving faithfulness just for her. Live your life as if you are already hers, as if you are already "taken." And whenever you become restless in your commitment, wondering if she will ever arrive, harness your passion for her into a love letter. Write to her that you are waiting, that you are loving her, protecting her, and serving her even now. What a romantic and heroic gift those love letters will make on your wedding night.

A complete man is a warrior poet who protects and serves both the covenant Life he shares with his King as well as the innocence and beauty of true womanhood. This is the kind of man that most women today hardly dare dream exist. Let's awaken the warrior poet within us and make their dreams come true.

> *"My beloved is all radiant and ruddy,*
> *distinguished among ten thousand.*
> *His head is the finest gold....His arms are rounded gold,*
> *set with jewels. His body is ivory work....*
> *His appearance is like Lebanon, choice as the cedars.*
> *His speech is most sweet, and he is altogether desirable.*
> *This is my beloved and this is my friend."*[16]
> SOLOMON'S BRIDE

III

FORGING
THE WARRIOR

8

The Christ-Built Soldier

Redirecting the Warrior Instinct

ust as young girls dream of being princesses, young boys dream of becoming warriors. When I was eleven I used to spend my time (while I was supposed to be doing my homework) imagining how I could rescue my school if it were to be taken over by "bad guys." I had a rather intricate scheme that I cooked up.

My strategy was to somehow escape from the screaming puberty-stricken crowd and crawl up into the rafters of the gymnasium. Because it seemed logical to me that the bad guys would herd us all like cattle into the gym, I crafted my war plan around this assumption. Like a lion-hearted monkey, I would carefully make my way through the rafters until I was just above the head of the lead bad guy. Cindy McFarland would look up and notice me, and I would delicately place my finger in front of my mouth as if to say,

"Shhhh, be very quiet. Your hero has arrived!" Then while the entire student body looked on in absolute wonder, I would fly down from the rafters and knock the head bad guy senseless. And then with a few Karate Kid-like kicks (I imagined that I knew karate, too) I would take out the rest of the bad guys. The entire student body would erupt with applause and carry me out (on their shoulders, of course) to meet the TV news anchors. In the end, Cindy McFarland would rush to my side and sigh, the way only a heroine can, "Eric Ludy, you are my hero!"

◦⁓

The desire to be a warrior is woven deep into the fabric of a man's being. We turn tennis rackets into machine guns and ski poles into swords (or was that just me?). We love Super Soakers and water-balloon launchers, and for some odd reason, we love to watch a snowball hit someone right smack in the nose. As young men, we have the desire to be great soldiers, even the instinct to fight and protect. So why don't more of us grow up to become true warriors who fight against injustice and protect the weak?

As young boys, we are like molten steel. At an early age, we can be shaped and forged into something valiant and heroic. But every time we don't stand up for the little kid getting picked on, every time we fail to befriend the new student with a funny foreign name, every time we don't take hold of the opportunities to protect our mother and sisters, we fashion ourselves into a decorative piece of empty manhood.

We are all too often forged into diamond-studded swords showcased in grandma's china cabinet or steel hammers comfortably lounging in jewelry boxes. We become useless for battle.

We want to be warriors, but we simply don't know how to begin.

On the Cusp of Wimpiness?

Maybe you, too, grew up a wimp instead of a warrior. And by that I don't mean you didn't have guts or weren't a tough guy. Maybe you played football, grunted off the agony of a dislocated shoulder, and returned to the game to score the winning touchdown. Maybe you raced dirt bikes, landed on your head, cracked two vertebrae, and never mentioned it to anyone. Well, you may be a tough guy, but that doesn't make you a warrior.

A guy can shrug off the pain and deny his need for medical attention, though his leg has been all but amputated, and still be a true wimp. A man may be willing to fight, persevere, and endure pain; but a true wimp knows only how to fight, persevere, and endure pain for one thing: his Self. A true wimp may fight to protect his own interests, but he cowers when the interests of others are at stake.

Growing up, I was a valiant protector of my reputation and my image, and I tried hard not to cry when my face slammed into a pad of concrete after my amazing dirt bike jump went awry. But when it came to protecting or fighting for anything outside of me, my Self, and I, in reality I wasn't much of a man. I was pretty much a wimp.

I did have my noble moments, however. When I was eight I yelled at Billy-the-bully Yarden to stop picking on little Timmy Valdez. But I was thirty feet away, hidden behind a big slide. Then there was the time in seventh grade when I compassionately chose to sit next to smelly Doug Torstenbo at lunch and had a fascinating conversation with him about Grape Fruit Roll-Ups. Of course, I never did it again, but I still felt it was a monumental achievement.

When it comes to sports and food, I have always been a loudmouth warrior. I have gallantly fought for "truth and justice," going to extreme measures to prove that John Elway was the best quarterback ever to play the game, that Randy Gradishar deserves to be in the Hall of Fame, that Canadian bacon and pineapple are the pizza toppings of choice for the true gourmet palate, and that raw cookie dough has been falsely accused of contributing to salmonella poisoning.

During my freshman year at college, I got into a wrestling match (I thought I was too dignified to fist fight) with Justin Winslow, the kicker on our football team. In the middle of a Monday Night Football matchup between the Denver Broncos and the Washington Redskins, Justin actually had the gall to shout, "Gary Kubiak stinks!"

How dare he?! Gary Kubiak, the Broncos' second-string quarterback behind John Elway, lived a quarter-mile from my parents' home back in Colorado, so I felt a special and deeply personal connection with him. Justin might as well have been insulting my mom.

"You take that back!" I barked, glaring at Justin over a huge bowl of cheese puffs.

"No way! Gary Kubiak *stinks!*" Justin repeated, with even haughtier disdain.

The rest of the story is a rather unpleasant display of my warrior instinct gone awry. In defending Gary Kubiak's honor, my uncaged animal passion somehow enabled me, the skinny golfer, to send the sturdy Justin Winslow limping off to the chiropractor's office.

For some reason I was courageous and daring when it came to meaningless things like football games and choice of pizza toppings, but I was an absolute wimp when it came to fighting for anything that really and truly mattered. I formed a lot of "wimpy" habits over the years, and as a result, my adult pursuit to become a courageous soldier of the Cross hasn't been an easy one. Retraining my warrior instinct has been like learning all over again how to hold a fork properly, chew with my mouth closed, and change my underwear daily. But the good news is that even as adults, we *can* be retrained. There is still hope for us spineless wimps to be transformed into heroic warriors, fighting for causes that have eternal value.

∽

For the last eleven years I have focused intently on building the courage muscles within my soul and the compassion muscles within my heart. After spending most of my life protecting my image and preserving my reputation, fighting for the Denver Broncos and going to battle for the virtues of cookie dough, it's not easy to *totally switch* the direction of the war. It's odd and uncomfortable to begin fighting new battles that actually might *hurt* my image and reputation (or make it appear that I'm wavering in my support of the Broncos and Canadian bacon).

I have begun to think completely differently about what is worth protecting. When Christ rules within my soul, I learn to see what He sees. He sees the little people that have no one to defend them. He sees the outcasts who have no one to befriend them. He sees the need to protect the innocence and beauty of womanhood. And most importantly, He sees the value of aggressively preserving the covenant Life within my soul.

If you are like me and you weren't properly trained in how to direct your warrior instinct, all is not lost. Warrior training is a natural outgrowth of the covenant Life. When God is invited into a man's life, He first of all establishes His rule over the man's soul. The very next thing He does is to *establish His military defense* within the man's soul. He trains our warrior instinct to become that military defense, protecting and fighting for Him.

> I have begun to think differently about what is worth protecting.

God is eager to run us through His warrior training course. This course consists of two phases of practical training. The first phase is internal, and the second is external. The rest of this chapter and the next will cover these two phases of practical training:

1. Learning to protect the King's Life within us.
2. Learning to protect the King's interests in this world.

If you are longing to be forged into a Christ-built warrior, read on. In the coming pages we will get down and dirty in the trenches. We will smudge on heavenly war paint and charge the fields of Bannockburn together. We will learn how to redirect our warrior instinct to transform not just our own lives, but also the lives of those around us.

When the Spirit of Almighty God possesses a man and the covenant Life brews within his soul, it isn't long before the nature and character of God are evidenced in his attitude, behavior, and lifestyle. God Himself is a warrior and a champion for the covenant Life and for truth and justice, and so we must be also.

When we get to know our God, we learn to fight His battles.

First Priority of a Warrior: Protect the Covenant Life Within

This is where a Christ-built warrior begins his training. After all, what is a warrior without his commander and chief, his weapons, his battle plan, and his fatigues? A warrior minus his covenant Life is like a soldier fighting a nuclear war with a feather duster. A warrior must learn how to protect the Life of our Commander and Chief within his soul.

The covenant Life is the one dynamic ingredient that sets Christ-constructed men apart from all the male counterfeits. Covenant Life is the source of all true greatness in a man—

the very root of all true heroism and righteous courage. Our covenant Life is the very power of God alive and at work in the human shell of a man. *For this reason, <u>our covenant Life is both Satan's greatest threat and primary target.</u>*

Satan has been around a long time, and he is a master deceiver. In order to protect our covenant Life with Christ, we must first of all understand what we are fighting against. We must know that our soul will come under ceaseless enemy attacks, and we must be aware of our enemy's tactics.

Satan has four tried-and-true strategies for snuffing out the Life of God in our souls. Let's look at each of these tactics so that, as warriors, we will be prepared to recognize and defend our souls against them.

ENEMY TACTIC #1: *To Drug Us*

His name is Darren. And he was drugged.

Just six months ago, Darren was pursuing God and eager to know Christ in a deeper way. He was attending a weekly Bible study and seeking to bring the Truth of his King into his daily life. "I really want God to take control of my life," he was overheard saying at the Bible study last fall. "I'm hungry for more of Him."

This radical Christian behavior was threatening the rulership of Self in Darren's soul. So Satan was notified of this potential danger and immediately went to work on Darren's life. The enemy introduced Darren to the computer gaming world and helped him to find the game *Everquest*. There was nothing particularly immoral about playing the game, but Satan knew Darren's weakness.

Gaming was the chink in Darren's spiritual armor.

For the past five months, Darren has found himself hopelessly lost in an imaginary world, fervently in search of "level sixty." He admits to playing up to fifteen hours a day. "I wake up at five and play until I leave for work. When my boss isn't looking during the day, I connect to the server and play. I play until two in the morning every night. This game is so awesome. I'm totally addicted, man!"

For Satan to win Darren back over to the side of Self, he didn't have to get Darren to commit some terrible crime. All Satan had to do was drug him with a seemingly harmless activity. Self has regained control of Darren's life, and Darren doesn't even realize that the Life of God he was so excited about cultivating is now strangely missing.

Satan's ability to drug us is a finely honed art. He doesn't always use computer games. Sometimes it's sports, music, television, movies, hunting, or even money. It could be any of a thousand things—all harmless in and of themselves, but things that may well be the "chink" in our armor.

We all have different weaknesses, things we are prone to idolize and worship. These are preoccupations that overtake us and become the focal point of our lives, drugging us so that we don't recognize the shrinking of God and the inflating of Self within our souls.

ENEMY TACTIC #2: *To Defile Us*
His name is Brian. And he was defiled.

Just three years ago, Brian graduated from Bible college with a passionate love for Christ and a huge heart for kids. He was hired by a church in the Midwest as a youth pastor and quickly became a success. He was fun loving and high energy—everything the church staff and the parents of the kids he worked with had hoped for.

This passionate Christian behavior threatened the rulership of Self in Brian's soul, so Satan was notified of this potential danger and quickly went to work on Brian's life.

Satan spied out Brian's weakness for anything female and carefully labored to assist Brian in discovering pornography on the Internet. After hours, when the church staff had all gone home, Brian found himself strangely drawn to his computer terminal. At first it was just a lust-driven fascination. Then it became more than just intrigue; it became a necessity—an addiction. Brian would spend hours under the hypnotic power of the sleazy pictures. He spoke out against pornography to his youth group, yet here he was, ensnared in the very things he said were wrong. His mind screamed for him to stop, but he felt powerless to change.

It wasn't long before his addiction began to whittle away at his relationship with God. He didn't feel like He could face Jesus anymore. *After all, how many times can God forgive you for something?* he reasoned. Then it began to compromise his messages to his kids. He began to weaken his presentations of Truth and dilute his message of a Christ-ruled life. How could he share about something that he couldn't live out in his own life?

For Satan to win Brian back over to the side of Self, he didn't have to remove him from church leadership or get him to stop talking about the things of God. All Satan had to do was defile Brian's soul. Self has regained control of Brian's life, and Brian can't face his God to hear the Truth anymore. *And Brian is still a youth pastor.*

Satan knows that if he can just get us to give in to temptation, he can begin to wrap his slimy fingers around our spiritual throats. It's not always pornography that he uses on young men. Sometimes it is lies or stealing or an addictive stimulant. There are thousands of little things that Satan can and will use to stain our soul. He knows that little black sins and the covenant Life cannot coexist. If he can subtly multiply the one, he is sure to eradicate the other.

Enemy Tactic #3: *To Delude Us*

His name is Ray. And he was deluded.

Ray gave his life to Christ three years ago at an evangelistic crusade. He got hooked up with a local church, spent a few months excited about the things of God, and even went on a short-term missions trip to Haiti. "I'll serve God in whatever way He asks me to," Ray was quoted as saying when he returned home, brimming with the excitement of his Haiti trip.

This radical Christian behavior was threatening the rulership of Self in Ray's soul, so Satan was notified of this potential danger and quickly went to work on Ray's life.

Ray met Barry, a middle-aged man who wanted to get him in on the ground floor of a multilevel marketing company. "It's the chance of a lifetime!" Barry said. "In a few years you will be driving the nicest cars and sipping piña coladas on the beaches of Cancun."

Barry called himself a "Christian," and therefore Ray assumed that Barry had Christ's interests in mind. At first, Ray couldn't see how this whole "business thing" fit with his passion for the poor and lost souls in Haiti, but as Barry continued on with his "Christian" reasoning, Ray soon caught hold of the vision. "Ray, just imagine," Barry declared with fire in his eyes, "if you spend just three years focused on this business, you'll be able to buy Bibles for everyone on the island!"

Barry continued deluding Ray with brilliant deftness. "God's plan for you, Ray, is to make you happy, and that means you need money." Barry's sales technique was well thought out and very appealing. "Ray, first God wants you to make your fortune, and then God will help you share that financial blessing with others."

Barry even persuaded Ray to start attending his church, which was full of other "fortune-hunting Christians" like himself.

For Satan to win Ray back over to the side of Self, he didn't have to get Ray to stop believing in Jesus Christ; he just needed to convince Ray that he could serve Christ while Self ruled his life. Strangely, Ray never did make it back to Haiti. All Satan had to do was delude Ray—twist the truth to the point that it lost its power to run his life. Self has regained control of Ray's inner command center, yet Ray now believes that this Self-ruled life is what God intended for him all along.

One of Satan's favorite methods of destroying the Life of God within us is to delude us. Very subtly he alters the truth, twisting it so very carefully, until it still *sounds* right but produces an opposite result. Throughout history, Satan has ruined lives with this sly tactic. He knows that if he can cause us to think we are serving God when in actuality we are serving Self and allowing sin to rule our life, we are both harmless to his plans and destructive to other Christians around us.

ENEMY TACTIC #4: *To Distract Us*

My name is Eric Ludy. And I was distracted.

At different times in my life I have been drugged, defiled, and deluded. But one of Satan's most convincing victories in my life occurred when he distracted me.

Leslie and I began a Christian ministry nearly eight years ago. We didn't intend to start it; it sort of started itself. Now eight years later, we can hardly believe what God has done. We have seen the lives of thousands of young people eternally changed because of this ministry.

But in the midst of it all, Satan attempted to destroy in us the very thing we desired to plant in our listeners—the covenant Life.

Our ministry grew so quickly that it overwhelmed us with busyness. Around the clock we were putting out fires, answering questions, and dealing with relationship minefields. We were teaching people how to put Christ first and build their entire lives around Him. Meanwhile, Leslie's and my time with Christ began to shrink. "When we get this next project done, we'll get back into the groove with God," we would encourage each other. But that "next project" turned into three hundred more "next projects" and years would pass before we recognized that the cycle would never end.

We were so distracted with the countless e-mails and piles of administrative duties that we didn't recognize the subtle maneuverings of Satan in our souls. We were so tired from living out of a suitcase on the road that our physical bodies were emptied of the ability to focus on God. Our schedule became so discombobulated from the constant travel that we lost any sense of spiritual discipline. This ministry, the very tool crafted to build the covenant Life in others, had become the weapon Satan was using against us to break down our own covenant Life with our King.

> If Satan can keep us busy, focused on everything but our King, our souls will fall into disrepair.

Self had slithered back onto my throne, and I hadn't even noticed. I was too distracted with the activity churning around me.

Distraction is one of Satan's favorite techniques to use on American Christians. If he can get us busy, focused on everything *but* our King, he knows that our souls will fall into disrepair. The covenant Life thrives on daily attention and grooming but shrivels up when ignored. If Satan can distract us, our intimate garden of fellowship with our King will soon become a tangle of weeds.

Satan utilizes these four tactics daily against our souls. He knows that if he can destroy our covenant Life, he will destroy our manhood. And that is why our covenant Life must be protected and preserved at all costs.

We have not been taught how to fight for the covenant Life. Many of us didn't even know it existed before reading this book, let alone how to guard and protect it. A great man not only has a covenant Life with his King; he will do what is necessary to protect and preserve this covenant Life.

Protecting the Covenant Life: Our Artillery for Battle

To defend ourselves against enemy attacks, we must have a battle-sensitive mind. That means being on constant alert, trained to recognize the subtle maneuverings of the enemy, and equipped to detect holes in our own armor and quickly fill them.

We must be transformed from attackees into attackers. In other words, we can't wait around for Satan to try and drug us, defile us, delude us, or distract us. We need to take the *offensive* against all that threatens to destroy our covenant Life. We need to launch a preemptive strike against enemy terrorism. We need to declare war on all that threatens to destroy the Life of the King within our soul.

To ensure the stability and strength of Christ's Life within us, let's look briefly at *five key military maneuvers* that we, as young men, need to learn to utilize in our lives. This is by no means an exhaustive list, but it is sufficient to point us in the right direction.

MILITARY MANEUVER #1: *Get to Know Our Commander*

Strength in the internal unseen battle begins with leaning on the strength of our King. When we try to live uprightly in our own strength, we will fail. Without His Life within, we are helpless and unable to perform as warriors for righteousness. But *with* His Life within, we are more than conquerors.

Intimacy with our King is a lifelong adventure of discovery and beauty, but it starts with daily taking time to kneel before His throne. It involves learning to listen to His voice, think His thoughts, love what He loves, and hate what He hates. As A. W. Tozer said, "Those who would know God must spend time with Him."[17] The warrior who is personally acquainted with his King, filled to the brim with his King's very Life, is a mountainous force to be reckoned with in the spiritual realm.

Many of us who have grown up in Christian homes think we know Jesus Christ. But knowing *about* Him and really *knowing* Him are completely different things. In a later chapter, we will discuss practical ways we can develop a daily, passionate, intimate relationship with our King.

Knowing our Commander is vital. Without His Life within us, the rest of our artillery becomes useless and impotent.

MILITARY MANEUVER #2: *Map Out Our Battle Strategy*

Satan will *never* let up. He is out to destroy us completely. But the covenant Life within us is an offensive weapon against Satan's kingdom and must be used as such. We must map out our battle strategy even before the missiles start flying. Then the next time Satan attacks with spiritual drugs, defilement, delusion, or distraction, we'll be ready to hit him where it will hurt. If we want to hit Satan hard, we must go after his spiritual prisoners, his POWs (prisoners of war).

Let me give you an example of a battle strategy that I have found super-effective in the protection of my soul. This strategy involves three key ingredients:

1. An identified point of attack.
2. A POW targeted for rescue.
3. A constant readiness to fight and fight hard.

First let me explain what I mean by an "identified point of attack." Ask yourself, *Where is it that Satan likes to attack me?* Does he tempt you with pornography? lust? lying? stealing? drinking? This is the "point of attack," the weak point you can expect Satan to be coming after. Next, target a POW for rescue. This is a non-Christian in your life who has yet to find the covenant Life of Christ—he or she is a prisoner of the enemy. When you have your "point of attack" and targeted your "prisoner of war," you are then ready for the battle.

The next time Satan strikes you at your point of attack, it is at that precise moment that you dive headlong into the enemy lines and go after your targeted POW. When the temptation comes, immediately start praying for your non-Christian friend. Pray that he would encounter Christ in all His fullness and that he would find a thorough and radical liberation from his Self-driven life.

The principle of this strategy is this: When Satan hits you in the chest, you hit him below the belt. Make him writhe with pain every time he tries to injure your soul.

Several years ago, before Les and I were married, I lived with my sister in Michigan. My weak point, at that particular period of time, was frustration. Nearly every day, I found myself irritated and on edge over something, and most often I took out my frustration on my sister. All too often, I would begin the day with insensitive words that created tension between Krissy and me. This was Satan's "point of attack." So I instituted the above-mentioned battle strategy. I started praying for our next-door neighbor, Charlie, every time Satan attacked my weak point. Since my struggle with frustration was rather intense, Charlie was prayed for *every day*. There was an immediate improvement in my relationship with my sister, and four months later Charlie found Christ.

Satan will back off when he knows that every time he hits you he will get hit hard in return. But this strategy will only work if we stay consistent in the battle. We can't fight hard one day then roll over and play dead the next. The covenant Life demands twenty-four-hour, red-alert vigilance. We must stay true to our battle plan.

MILITARY MANEUVER #3: *Resolve to Die*

One of the greatest hindrances to a strong soldier is the fear of pain and death in battle. The same is true for the warrior of the soul. Most young men are desperately afraid of what death to their Self would mean if it were to last a lifetime. The complaints of Self are many and frequent. *I don't know if I could live without ever getting drunk again! I don't know if I could live without ever watching porn again!* As long as we feed our Self, the voice of Self will mutter and complain.

Many of us, as young Christian men, are willing to give up our drinking habit or our porn *today,* but we aren't willing to give it up *for all time.* It's the potential of "having it back some-day" that weakens us in the battle for the covenant Life. A soldier on the battlefield will be ineffective if his mentality is *I'm willing to fight as long as my life isn't endangered.* Commitment on the battlefield demands an inner resolve to die today and *never live again.*

A great and fearless soldier of the Cross knows that *he* no longer lives, but that the life he now lives is his *King's* Life. The true warrior counts all things, both good and bad, as lost for the sake of his newfound covenant Life with Christ. If we are to be courageous and victorious in battle, we must resolve to die before ever taking the field. A man who fears nothing but his Commander and Chief is truly unconquerable.

A man who is resolved to die cannot be compromised by sin. A man who does not fear the pain and death that the loss to Self's rule will inflict on his comforts, image, dreams, and ambitions is a man who is ready to fight.

MILITARY MANEUVER #4: *Take Out Enemy Communications and Command Posts*

Our enemy, Satan, must not be allowed to set up a command post or a communication center within our soul. He must not be allowed to influence our thinking, whether through propaganda against the Christ-ruled life or false information about the battle itself. Anything that hinders us in building our life completely around Christ and following Him into battle must be ruthlessly removed. The battle for the covenant Life cannot and will not be won if the enemy is allowed to sit in on our war counsel. The Bible says it point-blank: "If your hand causes you to sin, cut it off….And if your eye causes you to sin, pluck it out" (Mark 9:43,47, NKJV).

In other words, if going to the library inevitably causes you to end up in the photography section gawking at nude photos, then stop going to the library. If you need a book, send someone else to get it for you. Or if having Internet access leads you to pornography, then get rid of your Internet access. If you need something off the Web, either have someone else surf for you, or even better, invite your mom into the room to join you when you browse the Internet!

If your route to work causes you to drive by a liquor store that cries out your name, and five out of every seven nights of the week you end up stopping, then take a new route back and forth to work, even if it makes your drive longer.

If your late-night habits cause you to wake up rushed in the morning and unable to spend time with your King, then scrap your late-night antics and get to bed earlier.

If your friends are pressuring you into compromising situations and feeding your points of attack, then say *"Hasta la vista"* to them and look for some new friends.

The principle is this: We must not allow anything into our life that feeds our point of weakness. A soldier doesn't dance through a minefield any more than we should play with a live hand grenade. When the enemy's entry points into our soul are boarded up, it frees us to hear clearly the voice of our Commander.

> We must not allow anything into our life that feeds our point of weakness.

There is nothing noble or courageous about "facing temptation." Temptation is like nuclear radiation—it is not meant to be fought but is to be avoided at all costs.

MILITARY MANEUVER #5: *Join the Fellowship*

Satan is a formidable foe. Just as a single soldier would never march against a thousand, so a single warrior, fighting for his King, must surround himself with an armed force. He must join the Fellowship or risk being overcome by the enemy.

If you are like me, you were trained by the Brotherhood, and your battle companions up to this point have probably been good 'ole Brotherhood boys. But the Brotherhood, with all its sex appeal and muscle flexing, is nothing but a covert operation of Satan, attempting to replace God's original design for masculinity training and male bonding. The Brotherhood is a shameless counterfeit of the Fellowship.

The Fellowship is a sacred league of heroic men, whose lives are not their own but have been bought with the price of Christ's blood. They are men who fear nothing but their Commander in heaven. They are men who would gladly lay down their physical lives to protect and serve the covenant Life of their King in their souls and in the souls of others. The Fellowship consists of the noble, the daring, and the courageous—the conquering soldiers of the Cross.

To fight the battles that lie before us, we desperately need to embrace the Fellowship. We must seek out men who make the King their number one priority in life. We must search out fellow soldiers who are Christ-built and Christ-ruled.

I have about ten men in my life who challenge me to passionately pursue my King. These ten men are not all in close proximity to my home. In fact, a number of them live in other states. But they play a vital role in the protection of my soul and the preservation of the King's Life within me.

My buddy Ben and I meet once a week for breakfast. Our purpose is to cultivate the covenant Life that each of us share with our King. We challenge each other, fight for each other, and encourage each other. Ben doesn't allow me to stagnate, and he doesn't allow me to drop my gun—he is a soldier of the Cross inspiring me to fight and fight hard.

Make it one of your highest priorities and requests of God to find the local branch of the Fellowship in your area of the world. Unfortunately, these kind of men are rare these days. But nearly every church around the globe has Fellowship members. The important thing to remember is that not *everyone* in a church, or even in a church leadership position, is one of them.

You will recognize Fellowship warriors by their life and not just their words. They are those who live out the life of Christ—not those who merely talk about it. They burn for Christ and seek to protect and serve His Life within them above all else.

To be successful in the battle, we must join the Fellowship of the Cross.

~

The battle for the soul is fierce and lifelong. Only those born of the Spirit of God, built by the Spirit of God, and trained by the Spirit of God will prevail. Surrounding ourselves with religious icons accomplishes nothing. Chanting religious mantras provides no power at all. Hanging out in religious buildings around religious people will in no way protect and preserve our life in Christ. For our covenant Life to thrive, we must be forged into warriors. We must learn how to fight valiantly for the Life of Christ within.

> *"Be strong in the Lord and in the strength of his might.*
> *Put on the whole armor of God,*
> *that you may be able to stand against*
> *the wiles of the devil."*[18]
> PAUL THE APOSTLE

9

The Commission

The Sacred Call of the Emerging Warrior

 remember strutting around with Pete Blakely during the summer months between our junior and senior years of high school. We smelled strongly of Coppertone and rarely, if ever, put on our shirts the entire summer. At seventeen, the dreaded *tan line* was even worse than being called a "dork" by a cute girl.

It is truly embarrassing to reflect back on this time of my life, let alone share this particular story with you. Pete and I thought that we were so tough back in the summer of 1988. The word I wish to emphasize in that previous sentence is "thought." We *thought* we were so tough.

One of our main hangouts was the Reservoir—known to all us locals as simply the Rez. I loved to say, "Yeah, Pete and I went to the Rez today." It sounded totally hip and made us seem like we were "part of the action."

Pete and I had a certain attitude that we unveiled at the Rez. It was a super-cool, tough, sexy, deep-bass voice, nobody-better-think-of-messing-with-me nonchalance. It was our *Rez-look*. We figured it made us appear more attractive to the girls and more threatening to the guys. In retrospect, I'm not sure that it worked the way we intended.

One day, while strutting around showcasing our Rez-look, we ran into trouble. This was ironic, because our Rez-look was supposed to announce to the world that we were looking for some trouble, when in fact we really weren't. I mean, what would Pete and I do with trouble? The Rez-look was only a look—it wasn't real. We only wanted everyone to *think* we were tough; we didn't really want them to *test* our toughness.

"Hey you, #$@!&!@," a muscle-bound sun-tanner barked in our direction. "You just got sand on me!"

Pete had unwittingly sprayed sand all over the Rez's legendary ladies' man, Mr. Clean, when he picked up his towel off the beach amidst a small gust of wind. As Mr. Clean and five Mr. Clean wanna-be's fumingly began to rise from their tanning positions and move in our direction, Pete whispered to me in a panic, "They're coming after us!"

We quickly left our Rez-look in the dust and made for the parking lot and my car. "If we can just make it to the car…," I encouraged Pete as we speed-walked across the pavement, trying not to look like we were running. With the Rez-look now officially abandoned, we tried to scramble into my little red coupe before the Gang of New York arrived. But in my panic, I couldn't get the key into the lock.

The rest of that story is far too painful to share. Let it suffice to say that I ended the day with two very blackish eyes and a super-bruised ego. Pete, meanwhile, emerged from the incident with only the bruised ego. How he did that I may never know.

Since Pete and I had our reputations to preserve as Rez tough guys, we invented our own rendition of the sand-spraying incident. When we related the story to friends or family, we strategically left out the part about us scurrying to the car in panic. We transformed the parking lot scene into a Western showdown, saying simply, "We *met them* in the parking lot."

Thus, we were able to add a bit of heroic luster to a sorry tale. I also masterfully transformed the two blows I received to the nasal region, into "Yeah, I took two of his hardest hits, and it didn't even faze me!" By the time Pete and I had put our spin on the story, we were Rez legends—the very picture of warrior-like manhood.

The Brotherhood breeds counterfeit warriors, counterfeit soldiers, and counterfeit conquerors. The Brotherhood forges tough guys who drive Hummers and eat jalapenos for breakfast. But as tough as they may be on the outside, the Brotherhood produces wimps on the inside. It produces men cloaked in the Rez attitude, but stripped of the Christ attitude. It breeds young boys like Pete Blakely and Eric Ludy—boys in search of nobility yet totally unable to do anything beyond protecting Self.

⌒

Modern manhood is like Chip Wilson from the second grade. Chip loved all the girls. He tried to kiss them, lift up their skirts, and even marry them with Randy Huddleston serving as his minister.

One day in early spring 1979, standing behind the big slide in the playground, Chip made a heroic promise to little Paula Murphy. On condition of becoming her new husband, Chip pledged to protect her from the big bad Benny Matthews, who used to pick on her and pull her pigtails. "I do," Chip vowed.

With the ardent fervor of a man in love, the seven-year-old boy promised to fight for his lovely Paula when the battle came.

But when Benny Matthews came to pull Paula's pigtails and prove to Chip that Paula was *his* girl, Chip ran and hid in the hopscotch area behind a big green bush. When the crisis came, he protected his Self. Although Paula screamed, "Chip, I need you!" Chip was busy protecting his own skin. And he had already begun the search for a new bride—someone a little more low-maintenance. While hiding in the big green bush, he spied Melanie Brown looking cute on the hopscotch grounds.

The Brotherhood teaches young men to fight, but only so far as Self's image and honor are preserved. It builds Chip Wilsons who are full of promises and expectations of nobility, but in times of trouble, hide behind a big green bush.

The Brotherhood has told us that all we need is mud on our tires and a muscular chest. But mud on a man's tires doesn't mean steel in a man's soul. And a muscular chest doesn't mean there's Self-sacrificing nobility *within* that chest. The Brotherhood has lied and left us with the outward trappings of toughness and Chip Wilson, a skinny little fifty-five-pound weakling, scrambling about for cover inside our souls.

Manhood isn't mud on the tires and a muscular physique. It isn't the Rez-look accompanied by the Rez-strut. The Brotherhood has sent us in the exact opposite direction from where our King intended us to go. Manhood was meant to be where Christ is. Where Christ rules. Where Christ directs. Where Christ lives. Manhood was intended by God to be swallowed up in the Life of our King.

Instead of directing our warrior instinct toward defending valiant causes, we have wasted it debating over sporting events, pizza toppings, and Super Bowl commercials. Our warrior instinct still stirs, but it stirs at the bottom of a trash barrel when it was meant to stir up spiritual reformations and revivals.

God didn't create us to become decorative swords in our grandma's china cabinet. He crafted us to join a *real* army and fight a *real* battle. The Christ-built warrior is a force to be reckoned with. He is intimately connected to the King, unswerving in his loyalties, fierce in his dedication to his cause, and completely surrendered to His King's warrior Life. When his King feels, he feels.

> The Christ-built warrior is a force to be reckoned with.

When his King bleeds, he bleeds. And when his King opposes something, he opposes the very same thing.

A Christ-built warrior is a mere extension of his King's will. He's the hand that swings the King's sword, and the feet that run the King's errand. He is the earthly visible expression of the King's invincible Life.

I mentioned earlier the two phases of practical training that God must take us through as His warriors:

1. Learn to protect the King's Life within us.
2. Learn to protect the King's interests in this world.

We explored the first of these two phases, learning to protect the covenant Life within us. Now let's explore the second phase of battle training.

We must be trained to fight for our King's interests in this world. To do this, it is crucial we know what battles He would fight and what errands He would run. During the Crusades of the Middle Ages, warriors who were untrained and unacquainted with their King fought what they imagined to be God's battles, swinging what they imagined to be God's sword, and running what they imagined were God's errands. What they left in their wake was one of the most horrific stories of human butchery this world has ever known. And it was all done under the banner of Christ.

It is critical that as Christ-built warriors we understand what our King's interests are and avoid fighting our own human battles in His name. The Crusades brought death; the

Christ-built warrior brings Life, liberty, and love.

Since it is critical to first *know* the King's interests before we can protect them, let's take some time to learn what it is our King deems precious and worthy of a fight.

The King's Great Interests

Our God is the ultimate Warrior. He defends, champions, and fights to preserve those things He holds dear. Amazingly, the way in which He chooses to do that is through men who have wholly submitted to Him. He longs to raise up men who will know His heart and, therefore, lay down their life to guard His kingly interests in this world.

Strange as it might seem, physical health, financial stability, and physical liberty are *not* at the top of God's list of priorities for protection. The things God finds of interest are very different than what we hold so dear when Self rules our life. God does not make our own security and comfort a necessity to accomplishing His purposes. Countless Christians have been stripped of all they possess, thrown into prison cells, and even died horrible deaths. And the whole while God stood by, feeling their pain, even as He *allowed* their pain. He *used* their pain to make them stronger warriors. God's originals are not afraid of physical challenges the way we are when Self rules our soul. Where we would often raise our sword to fight, God's original drops his and patiently endures.

A Christ-built warrior must learn to see life on this earth

the way God sees it. God is interested in things that matter *eternally*—He doesn't go to battle to preserve temporal comforts. It's not that God doesn't desire us to have physical health, financial stability, and physical liberty. Like any loving father, He desires good things for His children. But above all else, He desires His Life to be formed within us. That is His primary interest, and whatever must happen to cultivate that Life within, God will allow.

Let's look at some of the interests of our King.

INTEREST #1: *Protecting the Covenant Life*
Protecting the covenant Life within our own soul is the first and greatest battle of a Christ-built warrior. Every other battle we fight ultimately hearkens back to this.

INTEREST #2: *Protecting the Message of the Covenant Life*
Since I was twenty-one, I have had a rather unique desire to become a clear and present danger to the armies of hell. While some men dream of being an actor or a football star, I dream of putting all hell on red alert. I know it sounds about as stupid as picking up a baseball bat, hitting a hornets' nest, and standing there to observe their response. But I see it differently. I see it as the evidence of Christ's Life within me. When God shapes me into His warrior, I know that the enemy will shake in his boots, because a Christ-built warrior is Satan's greatest fear.

So I dream of causing Satan to walk nervously about his den, wondering what should be done about Eric Ludy. I dream of waking up in the morning and having a loud siren go off in hell screaming out the warning, "He's awake! Everyone to your posts. The skinny guy who can't grow a beard is awake!"

To join the list of the devil's "most wanted and feared," all you have to do is become a soldier for the covenant Life. It's really that simple.

Satan is gravely threatened whenever a human hears about, receives, and cultivates the covenant Life. He doesn't mind if we learn about Jesus or even teach about Jesus, just as long as we don't learn or teach in a way that exalts Christ by removing Self from the throne of our souls. Satan has nothing to fear until Christ possesses and rules as King of our soul—that is when all hell goes on red alert.

Satan is out to either remove God's Truth from our lives altogether, or twist it just enough that it loses its life-altering power. A Christ-built warrior, intent on having his name cursed in hell, must not let that happen.

A Twisted Gospel

"There are three things that we here at Compassion Community Church will *never* do," proudly boasts Pastor Warnick from the pulpit on Easter morning. "We will *never* present a condemning message like some churches do. We will *never* make you uncomfortable or make you feel like you have to change. And we will certainly *never* emphasize holy living like so many legalistic churches do." With that he receives thunderous applause. Then with a climactic ring to his voice, he booms, "We are a *loving* church; not a militant one."

Pastor Warnick has all the right words to say. But his is merely a clever counterfeit of the true gospel message. With subtle twists to the Truth, he leaves his audience feeling "free and loved," even as they are being ruthlessly squeezed by the rule of sin in their lives.

Pastor Warnick says, "We will *never* present a condemning message like some churches do." The true gospel, however, exposes the rule of Self, the controlling power of sin in the soul, and reveals the fact that we as sinners *are* condemned. The rulership of Self offers us zero hope and can only bring us eternal despair. The gospel message of Christ, by its very nature, is designed to make us squirm on the inside. It makes our Self thrash with anger. But though the gospel causes pain to our Self and strikes fear of condemnation in our hearts, it does so only to awaken us to our helpless condition. The true gospel offers us a new Life—an exchanged Life—free from the controlling power of sin and the angry bite of condemnation. It offers us, through the death and resurrection of Christ, the covenant Life of our King.

Pastor Warnick says, "We will *never* make you uncomfortable and make you feel like you have to change." But Truth demands that we change—that we bend our lives and experience around its reality. God offers no partial adherence. We are either in or we are out. We can't be alive and dead at the same time. We can't be ruled by Self and Christ at the same time. And when the Life of Christ enters our soul, behavior, and attitude, our entire existence on the planet earth is transformed. *To know Christ is to know the power of change.* When we know Christ, we start to live differently, speak differently, and even think differently.

Pastor Warnick assures his congregation, "We will certainly *never* emphasize holy living like so many legalistic churches do." Holy living is not something any of us can possibly achieve, no matter how hard we try. Yet at the same time, holy living marks *every* soldier of the Cross. It's not something we earn, win, or somehow work up to; we simply receive it when we receive the holy Life of our King. <u>When our King is given the freedom to live within our soul, the holy nature and character of our King will be evidenced in the way we go about living our new life.</u>

It is impossible for the covenant Life to produce legalism, because the very nature of the covenant Life is *God* at work in us. Legalism is *Self* at work in us, attempting to produce the supernatural results that only "God at work in us" can produce.

Pastor Warnick, though he appears to be an advocate of Christ, is actually a roadblock to Truth. Rather than teaching hungry souls how to be free, he is showing them how to be imprisoned. By subtly twisting the Truth of the gospel, he advocates a counterfeit version of God's Life. As a result, he is a stumbling block and a barrier to those seeking to enter into covenant Life.

A Christ-built warrior cannot ignore the twisting of

Truth. It may not be our job to stand up in the middle of Pastor Warnick's service and proclaim, "This is a bunch of bunk!" But then again, it might be. Our methods of fighting for God's interests will be unique to each individual battle. Sometimes God wants us to fight through prayer; sometimes He may desire us to fight through loving and gentle discussion; and sometimes He may ask us to speak out boldly against something. The key is spending time at the feet of our King in a quiet listening posture. He will faithfully lead us.

The Point of Attack

"Eric, you spend far too much time focused on the church. Aren't you forgetting all the lost souls out there?" People have said or implied this to me countless times. But the truth is that walking into a church building doesn't save anyone. If that were the case, we can forget about evangelizing. Let's abduct unbelievers, tie them up, stick them in the trunks of our cars, and dump them off at church buildings. Just by pushing them in through the double doors we could have mass revival.

Since God is so interested in seeing the covenant Life cultivated within His people, it seems obvious to me that Satan would seek to corrupt the very environment in which that covenant Life is meant to be declared, encouraged, and assisted in its growth.

In other words, he will target the church.

And just as Satan conspires against us as individuals, he is out to drug the church, defile it, delude it, and distract it.

As Christ-built warriors, it is our duty to protect the church from these enemy attacks.

Recognizing the Counterfeit Messengers
"How hot is it out here?" I asked as I wiped a stream of sweat from my brow.

"Someone said it's 108 today," answered our youthful guide, who was wearing a T-shirt that read "My God Rocks."

With every step on the dusty path, Leslie and I anticipated more and more the cool shade and ice water awaiting us in the "green room" behind the main stage. About a half-mile away we could see our destination. In between us and our ice water and indoor plumbing was a literal multitude of people. Thousands of sweaty bodies were jumping up and down, screaming at the top of their lungs as a well-known Christian band played up on stage. As we got closer, the sound became more and more deafening.

As we made our way through the frenzied crowd, the band's latest song ended with a screech and a drum finale. The lead singer wiped off a river of sweat cascading freely down his face and neck and then tossed the soaked towel into the crowd of maniacal teenage girls, who clawed and fought for the hallowed piece of soggy linen.

"Christianity is a rush, man!" he barked into the microphone. The crowd exploded in a thunderous agreement. "Christ said, 'It's done.' Now we have some fun, and then we go home to be with the Son!" More outrageously loud applause, along with whistles, hoots, and hollers.

"This next song," he muttered with his thumb in his right pocket and his chest thrust out, "is for all of you that think Christianity is too hard. It's for all of you that need to wake up and realize that God doesn't want us to be holiness freaks. He just wants us to party in the Spirit!"

With that the band exploded into song. The lead singer screamed into the microphone, "Let's *party*, everyone!" The crowd again erupted and began to dance like headless chickens on Ecstasy. The sultry singer thrust his hips in a sexual fashion as if to say, "See, I know how to have fun," and the front row of girls nearly fainted.

The lyrics of the song went on to share how "we shouldn't worry about our weakness; we shouldn't stress about our sin; the work is done, so let's have some fun in this world we're living in."

Oftentimes, the greatest threats to the covenant Life are in our own Christian backyard. They are dressed in "Christian" clothing and make mention of Jesus Christ. They speak tidbits of truth, shrewdly mingled with subtle lies. Their message is one that promotes the life of Self, the rule of Self, and the indulgence of Self. The music group Leslie and I heard that sweltering day may call themselves Christians, but their message is the antithesis to all that is true and powerful in the message of the gospel. They are a threat to the covenant Life within others.

But to recognize a counterfeit we must become familiar with the original. As Christ-built warriors, we must develop a nose for sniffing out things not in alignment with our

King's nature and character. To do this we must become very familiar and intimate with our God. When we spend every moment of every day at our King's side, listening to His voice and meditating on His person, counterfeit messages become more and more obvious. As soldiers of the King, we must fight against sly deception that would masquerade as Truth. The enemy must not be allowed a voice in the fellowship of the Cross. He must not be given a seat in the counsels of God's people. A Christ-built warrior fights to protect the integrity of the covenant Life message. Let's start standing up for our King's Truth and put all hell on red alert.

Here are a few practical things that we can do as young men to fight for the message of the true gospel:

- *Get to know our King, so we recognize His battles.* Spend time with Him, with His Word, and with His people. A man closely acquainted with his King is a man fit to represent Him in battle.
- *Learn to fight battles the way our King fights battles.* He is patient, kind, and slow to anger. He is gentle when opposed and quick to forgive those who injure Him. His main weapon is love, which He uses ceaselessly and without reserve. There are times He uses a whip, but more times in which He uses a kind word. As we cultivate the life of the King within our soul, we will learn to fight the way He fights.
- *Don't ever assume someone else will stand up and defend the Truth.* We must be willing to be the one.

INTEREST #3: *Protecting Life's Underdogs*

Growing up I wondered if God cheered for the Denver Broncos. "If I pray for them, will God help them win?" I asked my dad as the Broncos prepared for a huge game against the San Diego Chargers. That's a theological question difficult to answer. Though I prayed ceaselessly for fifteen years, they still got blown out in four Super Bowls.

The question is, does God take sides? Well, maybe not in football. But in certain arenas of life He undoubtedly *does* take sides. He wants us to be fighting on His side and not against Him. On the playground of life, there are certain teams God is committed to. When these teams take the field, God stands up and cheers. And it is when we cheer for, protect, and stand up for the same people that we can know God is 100 percent behind us.

Who does God cheer for? Often, it's for those that nobody else is cheering for. God likes the underdog. Not the underdog in sports, but the underdog in life. He has a special spot in His heart for people facing insurmountable odds. God is the hero of the poor, the grace for the persecuted, and daunt-less soldier for the oppressed.

He is interested in people weakened by health problems, age, or disability. He's a guardian of those without family and friends. And He is a champion of men and women who exist on the fringe of society, rejected by the culture. Never doubt it; the eye of the Lord is on the poor, the persecuted, and the oppressed.

When we are weak, He is eager to wrap His powerful

arms around our feeble bodies and carry us. When we are lonely, He befriends and comforts us. And when we are outcast, He accepts us into His inner circle and loves us the way we need to be loved. He's the provider in our poverty and the strength in our suffering.

A Christ-built warrior has strong "compassion" muscles. He has trained his eyes to see the elderly widow, without family and resources. He sees the Down's syndrome child being bullied by heartless teenagers. He sees the foreigner unable to speak the language and unfamiliar with the culture. He sees the needy, the persecuted, and the oppressed—and he is ready to step up and help.

Penny McWilliam is one of the bravest people I have ever met. But I didn't recognize her bravery back then when I was thirteen and lurching into puberty. At that age, I really couldn't see very far beyond my Self.

"Hey, Ludy!" Shawn Durstenburg shouted at me. "Doesn't Penny Wheelchair look *sexy* today?"

It's moments like these that define our character. A helpless victim named Penny stood vulnerable in front of me. Hobbling along on her crutches, she had steeled herself to pass through the Cruel Zone of the hall—right past Shawn's locker. Penny had severe cerebral palsy, couldn't speak clearly, and could barely walk. Most of the time she battled the hallways of Grove Middle School in a wheelchair, hence the nickname Penny Wheelchair. But though Penny was the

bravest of us all, she was the most helpless to defend herself.

And then there was me, a thirteen-year-old hotshot desperate to protect his reputation, standing in front of her with my tough-guy image hanging in the balance. What was I supposed to do in a situation like this? Choose to stand up for Penny who couldn't help my popularity rating one iota? Or align myself with Shawn Durstenburg, one of the coolest kids at Grove? I chose in favor of my Self.

"Yeah!" I mumbled in sarcastic agreement, then let out a warbled and guilt-ridden chuckle.

At that moment Penny lost her balance and fell facedown onto the tile floor. She lay there helpless right in front of Shawn's locker. Shawn laughed, accompanied by a chorus of snickers from his nearby cronies—and so I laughed, too.

A warrior sees the needy, the persecuted, and the oppressed—and is ready to step up and help.

Penny's nurse, Miss Belfontaine, who accompanied her at school, came rushing out into the hall and, seeing Penny on her face and a bunch of boys standing over her helpless body, laughing, she screamed at us, "How could you? *How could you?*"

For years after the incident I asked myself that same question, *How could you, Eric? How could you?* When the battle came, I turned and joined the enemy and fought against my God. But I can thank my King for new beginnings.

When I was twenty-three, God reminded me of Penny McWilliam, whom I hadn't seen since middle school. I sought her out and discovered that she lived just a few houses away from Grove Middle School. I met her at her house, wheeled her down the sidewalk to a quaint café, and treated her to a scrumptious lunch. I felt terribly awkward, but I felt I needed to be to her now what I wasn't to her then—a picture of Christ.

"Go to ska—ool?" Penny mouthed at me as we were finishing up our meal.

"Uh, what was that, Penny?" I asked, confused as to her meaning.

"Go to ska—ool?" she laboriously spoke while pointing out the window toward Grove Middle School.

"You want to go to our old school?" I clarified in horror. Penny nodded happily.

I hesitatingly agreed to stop in at old Grove. I felt wildly uncomfortable as I wheeled her in through the front doors and into the lobby. I instantly felt as though I had passed through a time warp, and I was thirteen once again.

Penny pointed down the main hallway as if to say, "Take me that way." All the kids were in classes and the halls were empty, so I agreed to venture forward. The same old smell, the same old lockers, the same old feelings haunted me. Then, to my shock and chagrin, the bell rang.

Kids flooded the hallways, laughing, pushing, and bouncing off one another. The cackle of immaturity filled the air. The next generation of little Shawn Durstenburgs looked down at Penny with mocking glances and irritated glares. *But this time I stood with her.* And as I looked around, I suddenly realized that I was standing with Penny in the exact same spot where she had fallen, ten years in the past.

⌒

As Christ-built warriors we must look out for the Penny McWilliams of this world. Here are a few practical things we can do as young men to protect life's underdogs:

- *Avoid hesitation.* When we see someone in need of assistance, whether it be the opening of a door, the lifting of a suitcase into the overhead bin on an airplane, or something more serious like an accident on the side of the road, we must train ourselves to respond quickly without any hesitation. The moment our Self recognizes the needs of others, it works overtime to construct reasons why it wouldn't be right, appropriate, or necessary for us to help. But we must learn to submit to the Life of the King instead of the reasoning of our Self. Self creates the hesitation that often robs us of the honor of protecting our King's interests.
- *Predetermine to protect.* Before we even encounter those who are weak, lonely, outcast, poor, persecuted, or oppressed, we must become determined to stand up for them. Just as a police officer may predetermine to pull someone over if he catches them speeding, so we as young men must predetermine to protect those we find who are in need of a protector. If we wait to make the decision to protect until we actually see the need,

Self often gains the upper hand by reasoning why it would be too risky to our comforts, reputation, or image. We must choose beforehand to protect the King's interests.

- *Understand their world.* The more we understand and become intimately acquainted with life's underdogs, the easier it is to know *how* to assist them. And the more we understand their plight, the more determined we become to assist them. When we associate with those in need, get into their world, and climb into their skin, we will know better what they are fighting against and how to fight for them. We can spend a weekend as a homeless man, a few days in a wheelchair, or even a week without sight. As we touch their world, it will touch our heart.

In Nazi Germany, during the Second World War, something terrible happened to the church. They went silent at the precise moment they needed to yell the loudest. They threw down their weapons at the very time they needed to be fighting the hardest.

Adolph Hitler allowed the church to worship Christ and keep their services going as long as they didn't challenge or interfere with the Nazi regime or with their barbarous treatment of the Jews. Hitler warned that if anyone helped the Jews, they would be treated as one of the Jews. He appealed to their longing to protect Self and, in so doing, shut them up and stripped them of their weapons. So instead of fighting for the King's interests, German believers fought for the preservation of Self and somehow ignored the horrifying atrocities taking place only miles from their homes and church buildings.

One Sunday morning a worshiping body of believers was nestled comfortably in their church building, singing from their hymnbooks about the loving protection of their God, while a train packed with Jews passed near the church on the way to a concentration camp. Upon spotting the church and hearing the singing, the Jews began screaming for help. But the churchgoers only sang louder to drown out the blood-curdling cries, unwilling to hear the pleas of those in need.

May we, the next generation of leaders within the church, not turn a deaf ear to the trainload of weak, poor, lonely, outcast, persecuted, and oppressed passing by us today. May we be willing to help them and identify with them. That is the model of Christ. That is what He did for us, and that is what His warrior Life within us desires to do through us.

Counting the Cost

William Wallace fought against the unjust cruelties inflicted by the English armies upon his beloved Scotland. Dietrich Boenhoffer defended the cause of the Jews in Nazi Germany when the rest of the church sat in silence. Martin Luther King Jr. spoke up for black people in America when they were an oppressed people group without a voice. William Tyndale stood up for the Word of God, yearning to see it pure and untainted and available to the heart and mind of every living soul. These are just a handful of Christ-built warriors. All these men died on the battlefield, protecting God's interests. Wallace was tortured, decapitated, and ultimately dismembered. Boenhoffer was hanged by the Third Reich. King was cut down by an assassin's bullet. Tyndale was burned at the stake.

A Christ-built warrior isn't called to a life of comfort and ease. He is called to battle. Rarely will it be a physical battle on a physical battlefield. More commonly, it will be a battle where the weapons the enemy uses are public mockery, public ridicule, and public shame. Christ fought a great battle, and He was betrayed, falsely accused, tortured, mocked, stripped naked, and crucified before a gawking public. When we fight to protect the covenant Life and our King's interests in this world, we will inevitably be treated the same way. In fact, it is likely that in fighting for the things God loves, we will be made weak, poor, lonely, outcast, persecuted, or oppressed. And when society scorns us and runs the other way, God will draw intimately near and be our greatest comfort and aid. He will be *our* Warrior.

> *"Contend for the faith which was once*
> *for all delivered to the saints."*[19]
> JUDE

*"Guard the truth that has been entrusted to you
by the Holy Spirit who dwells within us."*[20]
PAUL THE APOSTLE

*"Religion that is pure and undefiled before God
and the Father is this: to visit orphans and widows
in their affliction, and to keep oneself unstained
from the world."*[21]
JAMES

10

The Champion
Becoming Her Hero

ot many grooms awaiting their wedding day get to hang out with the bride's father. I was one of the lucky ones.

For a groom-to-be, there is no better way to get to know your bride-to-be than by talking to the number-one man in her life—her dad. Leslie's dad, Rich, is very soft spoken and usually only talks when he has something profound to say. It was from Rich that I learned, at a whole new level, the importance of protecting a woman's purity.

We were sitting in a booth at Perkin's Family Restaurant when he passed on the following bit of fatherly wisdom to me. "Eric," Rich said softly, "women rarely verbally express it, but they deeply want a man to protect them."

"What do you mean?" I asked. "Like fighting off big scary bugs and karate-chopping burglars?"

But Rich wasn't referring just to the act of protecting a

woman from bad guys and villains with curly mustaches. He was talking about the kind of protection I didn't even know existed: defending the purity *within* a woman.

Rich continued between sips of coffee. "When a man becomes a student of his bride-to-be, he realizes *two* things." I leaned in, my curiosity piqued. "First, almost every bride-to-be has predetermined the amount of physical or even emotional intimacy she feels comfortable engaging in prior to her wedding day. She may never verbalize that boundary line to you, but it is important for a man to figure out, because it is sacred to her. In the heat of passion, she may temporarily push her boundary aside, but afterwards she will always regret that it wasn't kept sacred."

As I digested this, Rich went on. "Since a woman rarely voices her predetermined boundary line, she usually expects her man to instinctively know what it is." He chuckled, adding, "This is a common problem in many marriages. Women know what they want, and they expect us men to know what it is without telling us. And, of course, we men don't know to ask."

"So you're saying," I interjected, "that I need to make sure I search out what Leslie's predetermined boundary line is?"

"No, actually I'm saying you need to do something even more than that. The second thing a man observes when he becomes a student of his bride-to-be is that she doesn't just want him to *understand* her sacred boundary line; she wants him to heroically *protect* it. A woman wants her man to protect what is sacred within her—her physical and emotional purity. She doesn't just want him to gruntingly agree not to violate her boundary line. She wants him to eagerly protect the purity of their physical and emotional relationship together."

Rich studied me with a sparkle in his eye. "Eric," he said, "Leslie wants you to stand up like a knight in shining armor and defend both the purity of your relationship together as well as the purity *within* her."

As guys, we haven't been trained to protect femininity. We've been trained to conquer it. But the essence of a Christ-built warrior isn't just overcoming difficult obstacles (e.g., women with morals) but rather to *become* a difficult obstacle, standing in the way of all forms of impurity and injustice. A warrior doesn't complain about sacred boundary lines; *he gives his life to protect them.*

We've been trained in the art of love and romance as if we were gorillas learning the art of removing a banana from its peel. We learn not to smoosh the precious and tasty fruit; but then once we've wooed it out of its protective barrier, we devour it for dinner. It is high time we redirect our warrior instinct and become a woman's protector rather than her conqueror.

In romantic love, a Christ-built warrior learns the curvatures of his lover's heart, learns the vulnerable points and most tender areas of her feminine soul, and then positions himself to defend those points with his very life.

Men Move Too Fast!

When it comes to romance blunders, even in healthy God-fearing relationships, there is one blunder that Leslie and I see happen in young relationships as often as the sunrise.

Carrie, a twenty-two-year-old who has witnessed this blunder up close and personal, characterized it this way: "Guys just assume too much! You say 'Hi' and they take it to mean 'I do'!"

Heather, a twenty-four-year-old still patiently waiting for Mr. Right, remarked, "Are all guys that way? Are they all ten steps ahead of a woman's heart?"

Well, Heather, I'm happy to tell you that not all guys are ten steps ahead of a woman's heart—some are only seven! Yes, guys have a timing issue. Actually, if the world were full of just men, then our timing issues would never have been exposed. But since the advent of the romantic relationship, men seem to have an internal clock that is a little off-kilter.

More men have messed up a "good thing" by rushing the progress of a relationship than probably any other mistake, including leaving the toilet seat up. Once again, this is an issue that exposes the lack of warrior training today. A Christ-built warrior protects; he seeks to guard and defend that which is vulnerable. But most men don't know how to protect a woman's heart, because they don't realize it is so radically different from their own.

> A Christ-built warrior seeks to guard and defend a woman's heart.

Men, for the most part, are clueless when it comes to a feminine heart's sense of timing. Nowhere is this better illustrated than in modern marriages. Married women know that the time it takes to "make love" is an *entire day* (to prepare her heart, to warm her heart, and then be ready to pour out her heart). Married *men* on the other hand would tell you that it takes five minutes. (That's probably why many of them aren't "making love" very long after their honeymoon is over). A woman's heart is warmed slowly, and her physical senses are charmed over time, while a man can be instantly aroused, physically and emotionally. As Chuck illustrated for us back in chapter seven, when men use their own emotions and physical desires as the gauge for the progress of a relationship, they are usually met with a strange and inexplicable hesitation from their female lover.

At this point, nearly every guy I've ever talked with about romantic relationships answers, "Yeah, what's up with that?" Many young men don't seem to have a clue about the differences between men and women—other than the basic physical differences and the emotional stuff spurred on by some weird thing called estrogen. Because we don't recognize the massive degree of difference between the sexes, we also fail to realize the *significance* of those differences.

A couple of days before I was married, my dad talked with me about my future with Leslie and what I could expect. "To love a woman," he told me, "you have to first protect her and let her know that she is cherished." He then told me an unforgettable story about my great-grandfather and how he treated his new bride on his wedding night. When finally alone after the day's festivities, my great-grandfather whispered these words to the love of his life, "Darling, if you don't feel comfortable making love tonight, that is just fine, because we have an entire lifetime together in which to explore the beauties of sexual intimacy. I just want you to tell me how I can serve you as my bride tonight and make you feel treasured and adored."

"A woman pressured," my dad added, "is a woman empty-hearted."

If a guy pressures a girl to blur her sacred boundary lines—physically or emotionally—she may give in. But when the guy "wins" a woman that way, he will not attain the unhindered, trusting adoration of her heart. We can never become God's gift to women until we let go of our own interests to *protect* the sacred desires of a woman.

The Makings of a Beautiful Marriage

It would probably be shocking for 99.9 percent of young single men to find out that the physical act of sex isn't the central theme of married life. Oh, it's a part of married life— a wonderful part! But it is not *the* part, like we all assume it will be.

"When I get married, I'm going to have sex *every* night!" dreamed my buddy Ronny on our youth group's annual camping trip, as we lay in sleeping bags under the open sky.

"My wife and I are going to have sex right when we wake

up in the morning and before we go to bed each night," said Ronny's cousin Joey as he stared up at the stars.

"How many times," I asked with genuine interest, "are we physically capable of having sex in a day?"

"I heard that you can do it seven times," Ronny said, trying to recall the details from some movie he'd seen.

Joey and I just mumbled our approval. "Seven would be nice," we declared as we began to drift off to sleep.

When young men dream of marriage, we inevitably dream of having sex "seven" times a day. We picture our wives saying, "Whatever you desire, my tasty hunk of a man!"

But then, sometime after the honeymoon, we arrive at reality.

We discover to our shock that sex really isn't the primary focus of marriage. Sex is but a beautiful, occasional reminder of a couple's shared love. For some men, that discovery is a huge disappointment. Why? Because most of us haven't been prepared for the *true beauty* of marriage. We assume it's the physical act of sex that makes marriage great, when in actuality it is the beauty of shared love. Sex is but a garnish set on top of the whole scrumptious meal of marriage. Sex certainly adds color and sparkle, but it isn't by any means the main course.

When I was ten, I spent weeks jumping around the house like a grasshopper, eager to go to Grandma and Grandpa's farm to ride their motor scooter. I only visited my grandparent's farm once every couple of years. As the trip approached, all I could think of was that motor scooter. As far as I was concerned, I was going to ride it twenty-four hours a day during my two-week stay in Idaho.

My two weeks at the farm turned out to be two of the best weeks of my life. And strangely enough, I only rode the motor scooter twice—for thirty minutes a pop. Roaming the creek bed in my grandpa's scooter was fun, but it didn't hold a match to all the other things we did that summer. Grandpa took me every morning up to the Wilder Café where we drank coffee (I had chocolate milk) with "the boys." I read the paper at his side and talked "farming" with all the burly guys in flannel shirts. I became a regular cowhand. But that was just the beginning. I played croquet in their front yard, climbed their big tree, wrestled with their dog Sandy, and rolled down their big hill. It was the ideal spot for cowboys and Indians, and the perfect spot for throwing the football or Frisbee with my dad and brother. It was two weeks of pure little-kid bliss. But the bliss wasn't found in motoring around the creek bed on a scooter as I had expected. It was found in a hundred other little ways that all rolled up together made for a magical time.

The magic and beauty of shared love is exactly like that. It is the composite of all the wonderful aspects of romantic love rolled into one. When built and governed by God, an earthly marriage shines with a beauty beyond words to describe. Its majesty and marvel are certainly *enhanced* by the sexual act, but the sexual act is not what holds a marriage together. Love is so much more than spending twenty-four hours a day on a motor scooter.

There are times when Les and I just stare into each other's eyes and want to weep for pure joy, loving each other so deeply that it causes us to feel like laughing and crying simultaneously. There are times when we lie in bed and hold each other, not wanting to move ever again and disturb the perfect sense of completeness we have found in having each other at our side.

There are also those challenging, stretching times, when the crush of life weighs heavy upon our shoulders, and we lean on each other with a rock-solid confidence that we will surely always be there for the other. I can honestly say that after almost nine years of marriage, I love my wife more today than I ever have before. Our life together seems to get sweeter and more amazing with time. Les and I have found the beauty of shared love, and we must never lose it. In fact, as a Christ-built warrior, it is my duty to fight to protect it.

If we, as young men, think that the beauty of shared love consists mainly of the physical act of sex, we will fail at protecting the beauty of married love, because we will find ourselves guarding the wrong thing. Like Chuck, most men spend their entire married life fighting for more sex in their marriage, all the while allowing the beauty of shared love to erode away. A Christ-built warrior knows that the real fight isn't for "more sex." The greater fight and challenge through all the years of marriage is for *more intimacy*. Cultivated intimacy is what makes a marriage amazing and, ironically, is what keeps the physical act of sex alive in a marriage for all time.

To protect the true beauty of our union before God, we must be prepared to honor and cherish our wife—<u>both before and after</u> she comes into our life. We must learn to fight for our marriage and never back down when the fires of testing grow hot. A marriage will not grow beautiful on its own. It demands the constant attention of a warrior, battling to keep Christ in control and not allowing Self to creep into the sanctuary of intimacy.

Protecting the Essence of Intimacy

Intimacy demands cleanliness. Leslie isn't overly eager to cuddle up next to me when I return from camping in the wild and haven't taken a shower for four days. For Leslie to get close to me, she needs me to be clean.

As a woman, Leslie is greatly affected by her surroundings. Everything from the smell of our home to the cleanliness of our window wells matters to her. Leslie can't whisper "sweet nothings" in my ear, for instance, if she knows we have an ant problem under the sink in our bathroom. For Leslie to give herself in love, the environment needs to be without blemish.

As a Christ-built warrior, it is my duty to protect the purity of our shared love. One of the key ways I can do that is by protecting the purity of our intimate environment. I'm the official ant killer of the Ludy household, not to mention the wasp eliminator and spider exterminator.

I am the smell defender, too.

That's right. I fight all intimacy-hindering smells. Last year I purchased one of those Ionic Breeze air purifiers for our bedroom, which gives off the scent of fresh mountain air. And since I am historically the "bad smell producer" in the Ludy home, I am careful to deodorize *myself* as well, by showering daily and refraining from "gaseous activities" outside of my bathroom.

While the purity of our environment greatly affects the intimacy I share with Leslie, there is another dimension of purity that affects our shared intimacy in marriage a thousand times more powerfully—*the inward purity of my soul.*

Most men don't realize that women follow the eyes of their man to see what they are looking at and admiring. When a man's gaze lingers on the shapely contours of an attractive female or on a piece of pornography, it's like a knife stabbed into his woman's heart. When a man visually delights in another woman's beauty, it's almost as though he is bringing that woman into his bedroom and saying to his wife, "Sweetie, you wouldn't mind if we allowed Trixie to join us in our shared loved, would you?"

For intimacy in marriage to blossom, a woman must know that she is the *only* woman in her man's life. She needs to know that her man only has eyes for her. If she gets even the slightest whiff of a feminine intruder into the heart and mind of her man, she emotionally shuts down, rendering all intimacy dead.

Even before we meet our future wife, every time we allow the image of another woman's body to defile our mind, we mar the purity of our future marriage, not to mention our covenant Life with our King. As Christ-built warriors we must learn to jealously protect our purity—both before and after marriage. We must learn to keep our soul clean, our mind guarded, and our eyes focused on things that will nurture intimacy with our future spouse. To develop Christ-like habits in this area, we must begin protecting the purity of our mind long before our wedding day.

For most guys, this requires some severe change of habits.

I remember the young man from Missouri who told me crassly, "I've spent twenty-five years staring at girls' butts." We'd been having a discussion on guarding our hearts against lust. He added, "I can't just go cold turkey, can I?"

A soccer player from California protested, "I can't help it that there are pictures of half-naked girls all over the place! God understands that I'm only human, doesn't He?"

In this culture, men are allowed free rein for their eyes. Today, it is socially appropriate for guys to observe girls' bodies and even brag about enjoying pornography. Thanks to modern movies, TV, and music, it is now *hip* for a guy to be sexually polluted. Therefore, men don't feel the shame of demeaning a woman by staring at her body. We don't feel the heat of embarrassment when we are caught mentally undressing someone else's wife (or future wife) and enjoying her for our Self. Even in Christian circles, there is a general attitude that says "Guys will be guys—women need to get used to it." Our standards when it comes to purity of the mind and soul are horrifically low. Unfortunately, our lustful habits are preparing us to kill all hope of intimacy in our future marriages, as well as our covenant Life with our King.

If we desire to emulate Christ, we must develop *new* habits for our eyes. We must learn to instantly look away from the temptation of the female body, as a gesture of love to the woman we will one day spend the rest of our life with. It is an outright lie that "guys will be guys" and that men are destined to be consumed and driven by sex. Men are destined by God to be *consumed by love*. There is quite a difference between the two.

If we can learn to save our gaze wholly and completely for our wife, one of the great secrets to marriage intimacy will already be in place before we walk down the aisle. When we look at a woman, we must develop the habit of looking at her *face*. When a woman walks by, we must develop the habit of *not* following her with our eyes. We must be super cautious to avoid movies with nudity (even partial nudity) in order to protect our mind and heart. Nudity can quickly become "another lover" invited into our intimate sanctuary with our wife. If a sexually enticing billboard, picture, or magazine ends up in front us, in the brief second we have to make our decision, we must train ourselves to run from it as quickly as we possibly can. It will beat us every time if we stay around and try to fight it.

And even when our physical eyes are not involved, we must take a close look at our *mind's* eye—our private thought life. Do we allow ourselves to mentally act out our sexual fantasies? Do we feed our lustful desires in the secret caverns of the mind? Do we mentally explore the bodies of women as we drift to sleep at night? Though our future wife can't see what happens in the corners of our thought life, our King does. Each time we give in to lust, whether physically or mentally, we invite Self back into the rulership position in our soul.

As Christ-built warriors, we are responsible for protecting the purity of our souls—and thus the purity of our future marriages. As the King's soldiers, we must learn never to allow anything into the sacred sanctuary of our shared intimacy with our future bride. From deodorizing stinky smells to deleting sexual snapshots, we must be the defenders of unhindered intimacy with our wife—both before and after we say "I do."

There are countless ways we can begin practicing now for greatness in our upcoming years of marriage. Let's look at six practical things that can help us prepare for excellence in our future.

PRACTICE GROUND #1: *Stand up for Our Mom and Sisters*
"Dude, you would not believe what your sister did!" Pete Blakely howled on the bus one morning during my freshman year of high school. Instantly, I felt my face heat up like butter on a warm stove. My sister was considered a "Jesus freak" at our school, and being related to her always posed severe

threats to my coolness. I tried to act indifferent as Pete launched into his tale.

"When she graded my brother's English test," he said mockingly, "she put a *scripture verse* on the top of the page!" Pete cackled loudly as if someone had just told a hilarious joke.

I knew I could not let my sister's embarrassing display of Christian sentiment ruin my reputation. I curled my lip cynically and shook my head in disgust at my sister's very *un-hip* behavior. "Are you *serious,* dude?" I shot back scornfully. "Man, I can't *believe* her!"

I could have stood up for my sister that morning. But the thought didn't even cross my mind. I had my Self's image and reputation to look out for, and that was far more important than defending my sister's honor.

The way a young man trains as a protector of his family is the model of how he will be as a protector of his future wife and daughters. From an early age, we are taught by the culture to distance ourselves from our family members to protect our own interests. We might consider standing up for our mom or sister if she was being physically attacked, but most of us never think of protecting the women in our family in more practical ways.

If a young man learns to stand up for his sister in little ways—defending her against criticism, giving her his coat when it's chilly out, or making sure she is not left alone in a potentially dangerous situation—he will be well on his way to mastering the rare art of Self-sacrifice. If a young man will

Eric Ludy

think to take his mom's car to the local Shell station and fill up her gas tank before she asks, or if, when his father is out of town, he makes sure the front door is locked before he goes to bed, he will have placed the cornerstone in his foundation as a "femininity-protecting" man.

In simple ways, you can begin to cultivate your role as protector. When you have the chance to stand up for your mom or sister, don't hesitate, even if it causes damage to your image or pride. If you catch your mom or sister doing an errand that could potentially harm them or endanger them, offer to do it for them. Be willing to put off your own plans in order to serve them. If we can learn to be an excellent protector of our mothers and sisters, we will be off-the-charts amazing in marriage.

PRACTICE GROUND #2: *Put down the Toilet Seat*
Since dirty and gross things will seriously impede intimacy with our future lover, let's send the dirty and gross sides of our manhood packing. As a single guy, you may enjoy a good burp, allowing yourself the frequent emission of foul odors, or even wearing the same T-shirt for two weeks straight. But I can tell you now that those male attributes will *not* cultivate the beauty of shared love in your future marriage. As a Christ-built warrior, we must train our life to be a gift to womanhood. We must be willing to sacrifice our comforts and habits to provide our wife with an atmosphere that awakens and warms her heart.

The toilet seat is a great daily test of our protector side. It may seem like a ridiculously miniscule thing, but it can make a world of difference in a relationship. Lift up the toilet seat when you go to the bathroom, and put down the lid of the toilet seat when you leave. That simple rule is a secret that few men have ever grabbed hold of. Let's develop habits that make a woman's heart warm—not habits that gross her out. Practice now by keeping your dorm room or apartment clean and smelling fresh. It doesn't need to smell like flowers; it just shouldn't smell like feet. Practice making your bed daily and cleaning up the dishes after you eat. Keep your environment clean and tidy. You can even practice keeping your living environment bug free.

PRACTICE GROUND #3: *Champion Femininity*
Modern femininity is under attack. The Brotherhood has trained up entire generations to view women as mere sex objects. And even if we have left the warped ways of the Brotherhood, all too often we stand by and do nothing as women around us are sexually hounded by the Bobby Gilberts of the world.

A fifteen-year-old girl recently complained to Leslie and me about constantly being sexually grabbed and touched in the halls at school. A friend had told her to fight back, run the other way, or even deck the guilty males if necessary, but she felt helpless when more than one guy surrounded her. Why should this young woman be forced to fight against this perverted male harassment on her own? What if even one guy stood up to his male counterparts on her behalf? Such an idea is almost unheard of in today's world. It is even considered chauvinistic or antifeminist to stand up for a woman in our modern culture. But nothing is more pro-female than using our warrior instincts to fight for a woman's honor.

We must stand up and defend femininity. Obviously, this starts with our learning to view femininity through God's eyes. But the next step is for us to help other young men in this culture see femininity correctly. Just imagine if we as young men began to speak up for young women when we hear the Brotherhood boys talk perversely about them. What would happen if Christ-built warriors began training other men how to truly respect, honor, and protect femininity? The beauty and sparkle of marriage will skyrocket when men become champions of womanhood once again.

PRACTICE GROUND #4: *Begin Taking Responsibility*
As Christ-built warriors, we must take responsibility for the success or failure of our marriages. Since the man is designed to be the primary protector of intimacy, the responsibility falls onto his shoulders when anything divisive creeps into his home or marriage relationship. In an argument between a husband and wife, we should always be willing to take responsibility first for the disagreement, even if the fault is hers. As the protector of our marriage, we should be the *first* to ask forgiveness and the *first* to initiate the rebuilding process.

As young men, we can begin practicing this noble behavior even now. In arguments with family or friends, we must be willing to be the first to say "I'm sorry." We must, as Christ's representatives, learn not to complain and cast blame. We must learn to humbly appear to be the primary guilt-bearer to bring reconciliation. Jesus initiated reconciliation with us and, as our Champion, took our sins upon Himself. It is our duty as Christ-built warriors to bear the likeness of Christ as we relate to others.

PRACTICE GROUND #5: *Never Pressure*

To repeat my father's phrase, a woman pressured is a woman empty-hearted. As Christ-built warriors, we must learn to treat women the way God treats us. God doesn't force us into agreement with Him. Rather, He gently *invites* us into agreement with Him. Jesus Christ is the ultimate gentleman. He doesn't force His will upon us; He doesn't even pressure us toward His will. He simply woos us to His will.

Likewise, we must learn to treat women with gentleness instead of coercion. To protect and guard a woman's heart, we must learn to treat it differently than our own. Guys get excited quickly, but a woman's heart warms up slowly. Just as a grown man shouldn't sprint down the street holding on to the hand of a two-year-old, we must not forcefully pull a woman along emotionally and endanger her slow-moving heart.

As we've already noted, living patiently with our moms and sisters is a tremendous practice ground for marriage. If we can learn to be patient with our sister when she is getting ready in the bathroom and seemingly taking forever; if we can learn to really *listen* when our mom shares her feelings; if we can show patience and understanding even when their emotional displays seem completely illogical, we will be well on our way to being a strong protector of a woman's heart. Patience and self-control are two super-important weapons in the warrior's armory.

PRACTICE GROUND #6: *Guard Her Heart*

All too many of us have been trained by the Brotherhood to employ hunting tactics to relate to girls. We observe women covertly, discovering what girls are attracted to. Then we act out the part of the "sensitive male" or the "flirtatious heart-breaker" whenever the ladies are near. It feeds our manly ego to receive female attention. So we make sure to act in a way that will turn female heads and open female hearts. But what we justify as "a little harmless flirting" or "an innocent three-hour phone conversation with a female friend" can recklessly loose the heart and emotions of a woman like an open floodgate.

Many a young woman has spent many a night crying over a broken heart—not from an ended relationship, but from the *false hope* of a relationship that never began. As young men, we have the power to awaken female emotions and draw them to our Self, a power we often use at a woman's expense. We must be extra cautious as we relate to girls, even in casual friendships. We must carefully guard our words, our actions, and our physical behavior so as not to draw feminine emotions to us to gratify our own selfish desires. In protecting the emotions of the women in our life, we are helping to guard their hearts as treasures for their future husbands—and thus defending the heart of *our* future wife by honoring her with the way we relate to the opposite sex.

❧

Modern femininity is in need of a champion. Today's girls may not be asking for men to stand and protect them, but we *need* to, nevertheless. Men were designed by God to be defenders of everything beautiful and pure within the heart of a woman. We have been commissioned by the God of the universe to go to war to preserve the essence of what makes womanhood great. For femininity to flourish, for marriages to sparkle, and for little girls to skip about with innocence, true warriors are again needed. It's time to become that gift for womanhood we have always desired to be.

"Husbands, love your wives, as Christ loved the church and gave himself up for her...husbands should love their wives as their own bodies."[22]
PAUL THE APOSTLE

"I made a covenant with my eyes not to look lustfully at a girl."[23]
JOB

IV

SHAPING
THE POET

11

The Passion

Unlocking the Affections of the Manly Soul

en are machines!" we chanted in Brotherhood meetings when I was fourteen. "We are robotic automatons with large sexual organs to make up for the absence of a feeling heart."

"Amen," shouted the testosterone-riddled congregation.

"Preach it!" hollered a screechy voice from the back row.

The Brotherhood is sly. Sure, they don't actually have formal meetings, but somehow they communicate with us. Young men know the rules as though someone had given us a list to memorize. From an early age we learn to laugh and scoff at those who don't know the rules.

"Timmy Smits got hit in the head during dodgeball last period and is crying like a baby!" howled Shawn Durstenburg in a cuttingly derisive tone. The rest of us responded in kind with "What a wimp!" or "I always knew he was a girl in disguise." It hadn't taken us long to realize that real men don't cry. To be termed a "wimp" or a "girl in disguise" was tantamount to wearing a flowery dress to school.

"Did you see Jimmy Johnson pushing Penny Wheelchair down the hallway yesterday?" cackled Tory Nasland. The rest of us Brotherhood Boys laughed along with Tory, adding taunts like "Jimmy's such a girl!" and "He needs a bra!" To be termed a "woman" ranked up there with that dream of showing up at school in nothing but your underwear.

The Brotherhood trains us to lose our feelings at a young age. Sensitivity, compassion, and caring are branded as "wimpy" behavior off-limits to "real" men. Modern men must deny their heart and soul to become the kind of men the Brotherhood admires. But in doing so, they grow farther and farther from their King who is the only one capable of unlocking the true depths of manhood within them.

My Confession

When I reached the age of twenty, I no longer had to try to suppress tears or emotion; I'd reached the point where I just plain *couldn't* cry, even if I wanted to. After so many years of covering my true feelings, disregarding any hint of compassion for those less fortunate than myself, I *was* a machine. I still felt, but not in the way God designed me to feel. I got furious with referees during football games, for example. I got excited when a Broncos player made a huge play, and I felt horribly dejected when the Broncos lost the Super Bowl. But the true God-designed passions of my heart were stunted and retarded in their growth.

While I was attending missionary school in Texas, God confronted me on this issue. It was the spring of 1990, the very beginning of my covenant Life with Him. He knew that for my covenant Life to grow and flourish, my heart must be free to *feel* and live. I lay in my bunk, staring at the wood panels above my head. The room was filled with the sounds of various snore-types and the heavy breathing of sleepy males. God was working in my soul, and He felt very near and present.

"Lord, please show me," I softly prayed, "if there is any-thing wrong in my life that still needs to be made right." I lay there silently, listening intently for the gentle voice of my God as it pressed its message into the wet clay of my soul.

To describe the voice of God is like describing the rush of wind through your hair. It affects you without appealing to sight, sound, or smell. It moves you though it doesn't have a shape, a size, or visible strength. It's something *felt* more than heard. The voice of God is a sound discerned by the ears of the soul as the Life of God within speaks its divine language.

As I lay still within my missionary bunk, God opened my soul before me as a doctor removes the bandages to inspect the infected wounds of a man ravaged by a horrible skin condition. My soul was diseased and dying. Having spent years under the dictatorship of Self, it was emaciated from lack of spiritual food and bloated with the fever of emo-tional starvation.

"What must I do, Lord?" I asked, trembling in fear. "Show me what I must do to allow Your Life to completely fill my soul."

Each of us have our own personal roadblocks that keep the Life of God from growing within our soul. The roadblock in my life that God chose to point out that night was my tough, unfeeling exterior I had cultivated for the Brotherhood. Even though I was attending a missionary school and learning daily about Jesus Christ, I had maintained my steely attitude. I had encased my heart in stone and worked hard to convince the other missionary males that I was a card-carrying member of the Brotherhood.

Danny had asked me when I first arrived, "How much do you bench press?" I humbly stated my personal best—conveniently adding fifteen pounds.

"How fast did you say you ran the 400 meters?" Tyler had inquired around the breakfast table one morning. I confidently reported my best time—with four seconds shaved off.

The truth would have left me looking plain and unimpressive to these guys. The Brotherhood had trained me to serve my image and promote my reputation. I had to *add* to who I was, because I surely wasn't enough without it.

Now as I lay in my bunk, God was showing me what I had done.

"God, I'm so sorry!" I cried out in the dark as my soul was laid bare. "Please, please forgive me for my pride, for my lying, and for my fear of rejection." As I lay there motionless, my King touched me deeper, moving me in a direction that I feared. "Lord," I pleaded, "it is hard enough for me to face these stains on my soul in front of You. Please, don't ask me to do...*that!*"

The next day I arrived in class, still trembling from the previous night. I had slept little and battled intensely with God. I knew beyond a shadow of a doubt what it was that God desired of me. I knew what stood in the way of my soul being free to feel and live, and something had to be done.

I raised my hand.

Our teacher, Dean, acknowledged me. "Yes, Eric?"

"Uh," I hesitated.

The room was silent, all eyes staring in my direction.

"Uh, I need to say something, if that is all right." I desperately hoped that somehow it *wouldn't* be all right.

"Sure!" Dean agreed, much to my dismay.

I stood and, with wobbly knees, made my way to the front of the classroom. I stared at the floor for quite a few long seconds, waiting for the right words to enter my head. I wished that I could somehow say this in a way that would both obey God and preserve my tough Brotherhood image. But that wasn't possible.

"I've lied to you all," I gulped as my face turned burnt orange with embarrassment. The class remained inordinately quiet. "I've lied about who I am to make you think I am something that I am not." The image I had worked so hard to build and spent so many years protecting was crumbling—I never dreamed that I would be the wrecking ball.

Finally, after a few more awkward moments, I said, "Danny?"

Danny's eyes grew wide.

"Remember when I told you how much I can bench press?"

Danny nodded.

"It isn't true," I ashamedly admitted. "I added fifteen pounds to my real weight."

For most people, to acknowledge their accurate bench press weight might not seem too difficult a task. But it was one of the most humiliating and most excruciatingly painful things I had ever done. It exposed me for who I *really* was. It laid me open for rejection and the Brotherhood's disdain. But God was gently nudging me to continue.

"Tyler?" I said. "When I told you how fast I can run the 400 meters, I took four seconds off my real time."

Again the sting of humiliation and the burn of disgrace ate at my insides. What would this do to my good standing as a Brotherhood member?

I stood vulnerable as a man in front of the class. Everything that I had built my manhood around was now shattered in a pile at my feet. I was broken and humbled and was willingly showing *weakness* for the first time in my life.

"Please forgive me, you guys, for what I have done. I am so sorry!"

To my shock, the guys didn't scoff or stare with disdain. These guys were *true* comrades, not Brotherhood-built counterfeits. Without hesitation, they each stood up and came to where I was standing at the front of the class. In my weakness, when I was most vulnerable to rejection, these men embraced me, loved me, and forgave me. They wrapped their arms around me and said, "Eric, we love you—just for who you are!"

I had never encountered such bald-faced love and acceptance. I had done nothing deserving of love, yet they loved me. I had not a shred of dignity left, yet they accepted me. Emotion overcame me. In very non-Brotherhood style, I began to cry. Soon, the tears were falling so hard that my tough exterior vanished and my face contorted uncontrollably. I cried in front of the men who I had desperately wanted to see me as strong. I admitted weakness in front of them, and in doing so, my heart was set free.

For the first time in my life, I felt able to receive the love of my King. Through the unconditional love of these Christ-built men, my manly heart was invited into the realm of true and untainted passion. I was ready to be both a giver and a receiver of the amazing love of Calvary's Cross.

God has a unique journey planned for each of us—a journey meant to unlock the affections of our soul. He designed all men to *feel* like He felt as a man walking this earth. He designed us to be stirred to *passion,* just as He was.

When His covenant Life occupies our soul, our emotional world is totally remade. Where before there was a smoking crater there is now a radiant pool of world-altering love, mercy, and compassion. Satan fears the unquenchable power of the covenant Life. *He fears a man who loves like Christ loved.* He trembles before a man who willingly bends his knee to wash dirty feet. A man with an unlocked soul, yielding a harvest of outrageous love, is a tremendous threat to the kingdom of the enemy.

We have already explored the warrior side of manhood. We learned how to build and tone the spiritual muscles and cultivate the courage of a valiant protector. Now we will complete the picture of ultimate manhood by learning how to unlock the heart.

To *protect* our covenant Life is essential, but to *serve* the covenant Life leads to true fulfillment unlike any we've ever known. The warrior prepares the way for the lover.

> Satan fears a man who loves like Christ loved.

Becoming a Christ-built *poet* is the marvel and mystery and, ultimately, the destiny of every man. To not only swing a battleaxe, but also sing the sweetest of love songs—this is the destination of a man constructed out of God's lumber. This is what it means to be a warrior poet.

"Gentleness is weakness!" shouts the Brotherhood.

"Gentleness is the truest strength," answers the Christ-built lover.

To be gentle does not dull a warrior's sword; on the contrary, gentleness sharpens it all the more for battle. A man who is familiar with his heart and is able to cultivate passion within will fight more fiercely because he *feels* for what he fights.

Our King wants to train us to become great lovers—not just of women but, more importantly, of Himself and of our fellow man. But men have been trained to scoff at feelings and emotions. Growing up, I would have been horrified at the thought of anyone ever seeing me shed a tear. This posed a bit of a dilemma whenever I watched sad movies with friends or family members. During a heart-wrenching deathbed scene, everyone else in the room sniffled or tearfully dabbed their eyes, and I, too, would feel an awkward surge of emotion rise within my chest. But of course I couldn't actually *cry,* so my squashed feelings came bumbling out in a different way—I giggled. At the sound of my snorting giggles, everyone sitting near me would look my way accusingly as if to say, "What is the matter with you? How can you be so heartless?!" It wasn't that I didn't have emotion; it was that my feelings were imprisoned by my pride. And according to the Brotherhood, it was far better to be accused of being a heartless machine than a tear-stained wimp.

The God-constructed man does not have to hide his emotion. He is familiar with the terrain of his heart and is able to submit fully to the rulership of his fiery, passionate King. God *feels.* God has emotions. It is God's Life that brews within our chests. God is a great Warrior, but He is also a compassionate, gentle, and eternally loving Poet. His Life within us will produce nothing short of a nuclear explosion of amazing love within our hearts. A Christ-built man doesn't scoff at feeling, but *embraces* it as a touch of heaven within his soul.

Cultivating a Poet's Heart

To have a poet's heart does not mean to cry all day over soap operas or sad movies. A poet's heart is a mountain of spices carefully planted in the soul of a man by Christ. The spices grow more fragrant and more powerful with faithful watering and attention; but like any living organism, they can shrivel up and die without proper care.

This mountain of spices that Christ plants within our heart is a majestic representation of the very nature of our King. A poet's heart is princely and strong, yet it sings a lover's tender melody. A poet's heart is the symbol of ownership that God places upon our life when He gains complete control of our soul. A God-crafted poet's heart should be every man's pursuit.

The Spice of Tenderness

"Eric, dear," my mom said with a calculating look, "I have a question for you."

In the first twenty years and three months of my life, I had never purposely made myself available for a "mom" question. She was unwavering in her commitment to inquiring about the regularity in my changing of my underwear. On the subject of dating: "Okay, she is pretty, but is she a *Christian?*" Then there was my all-time favorite: "Were you the last one in the bathroom, leaving the toilet seat up and all nasal passages on red alert?"

I had spent my entire life avoiding "mom" questions. But

now, after encountering the Life of God full-strength for the first time, I found myself strangely open to an introspective question, asked the way only a mother can.

She said, "I promise it will have nothing to do with your underwear or the toilet seat." We both laughed, and I told her she was free to throw her question my way. She asked, "What attribute of Christ do you most desire to see formed in your life?"

She had pinpointed the very thing God had been nudging in my heart and mind. After discovering Jesus Christ in such a new and profound way, I was beginning to realize that there were practical aspects of His new Life within me that I needed to cultivate and water. And there was one in particular that was swimming around in my mind like an ocean liner in search of a port.

"Tenderness," I answered without hesitation. It was as if the answer was waiting to come out before the question was even asked. "I know God wants to teach me how to be tender."

My family had always referred to me as "the stiff board." The only time I ever hugged anyone was when it would be socially damaging if I didn't. Picking up relatives at airports always provided the opportunity to display my stuff. "Oh, Eric, it's great to see you," my grandma would say with a twinkle in her eye and her arms opened wide. "Now give me a great big hug, dear." Like a petrified piece of wood I would open my arms, lean my tense body against hers, and provide a wimpy squeeze with chopstick-like arms. I looked like a malfunctioning robot when I hugged people.

I didn't know how to be soft. I only knew how to be stiff.

"Eric," my mom would say, "you have to *relax*. When I hug you, I feel like I'm hugging a huge piece of peanut brittle that's about to snap in two."

In hopes that I would somehow learn to "tenderize" my exterior, my mom began subjecting me to "hug practice" sessions. Unfortunately, these well-intentioned lessons didn't work; they only made me more self-conscious about my hugging skills, which caused me to tense up even more in those situations.

It wasn't really a matter of needing to learn good hugging technique. My external stiffness was a direct result of my stiffness of heart. God wanted to begin the Eric Ludy softening process by first cultivating tenderness *within*. And it was my heart that God went to work on.

~

To most guys, the word *tenderness* sounds fluffy and cloud-like—something without much substance, like a billowing heap of pink cotton candy. In a recent discussion with a group of college-age guys, I asked the question, "What do you think true tenderness really is?" After a few moments of blank stares, a few of the guys ventured some guesses.

"Are you talking about steak?" a hefty linebacker said excitedly.

"Do you mean like hugs an' stuff?" asked another guy with a bright blond crew cut. I told him he was a little closer to the mark.

"Tenderness is a *girl* word," a guy with glasses offered knowingly. "It's like the stuff they watch in those chick flicks."

Once again, we guys are out in left field picking lint from our belly buttons. Tenderness is one of the single most important tools in the arsenal of a world-altering man, but most of us have never once associated it with masculinity.

Tenderness is the secret to winning a woman's heart, as well as the secret to cultivating God's heart within *us*. If Self rules our soul, then tenderness cannot exist within us. The first step in learning tenderness is *considering other people as more valuable and important than our Self*.

Everywhere Les and I go, we challenge ourselves to make people feel important. In fact, if we have enough time, we want people to feel like royalty. We don't always succeed at this; it's so easy to overlook others and focus only on our own issues. But when someone is treated like they're important, it can have a profound effect upon that person.

We like to target those who are most often overlooked and unappreciated. What if we actually started noticing the tired middle-aged lady serving us at the restaurant? What if we turned the tables and began serving *her* by expressing sincere appreciation for her help or asking how her day is going? Waitresses, cab drivers, and janitors all find it tremendously satisfying to have someone go out of their way to value them and treat their life and work as significant.

"Hi!" I said the other day to a guy getting out of his car at a rest stop. We chatted about his journey to Colorado Springs from Taos, New Mexico. We briefly discussed his interest in molecular biology, and then he trotted away to visit the concrete restroom.

When I got back into my car, I was asked by one of my buddies why I bothered spending time talking with a stranger at a rest stop. "You'll probably never see him again," my friend said, "and you didn't share the gospel with him. So what good did it do to waste three minutes chatting?"

Tenderness finds value in everyone, even if our own encounter with the person is only three minutes. Tenderness sees the potential glint of a royal crown shimmering from every forehead, and it desires to pass on a jewel from God's kingdom to every person we encounter, even if that jewel is a simple smile or a kindly "hello."

Learning tenderness means not only retraining our eyesight to see others as important, but also to see the *unique needs* of others. It's one thing to notice a man at a rest stop and say "Hi," but if the same man has a flat tire and doesn't know how to fix it, then we must be willing to move beyond the pleasantries and offer to help meet his need.

It's one thing to treat a waitress like a princess and serve her with encouraging words, but it is a whole other dimension of tenderness to become of student of her needs and help meet those needs. The long and short of it might be that she needs a generous tip to boost her spirits and help keep her going. Mere expressions of value toward someone are empty if our words aren't backed up with practical assistance.

His name is Drew. And he is learning tenderness.

Drew got married last year to a feisty young woman named Wendy. He calls her his "angelic wildcat." After twenty-eight years of singleness, Drew is still adapting to the idea of sharing his life with someone else. Especially someone who thinks, acts, and feels so differently from the way he does.

I'm proud of Drew. He was trained by the Brotherhood, just like I was, so the transition into a Christ-built poet hasn't been quick or easy. He is learning to see Wendy as his princess and, therefore, treat her needs, her feelings, and her desires as *more important* than his own. Any husband will tell you this is quite a challenge.

Drew is becoming a student of his wife. He's learning how she works, so he can serve her and love her more effectively. He keeps a journal of the things he's observing in her so he can continue to grow into a better husband. As Drew says, "I'm learning to serve my angel instead of waiting to be served by her, and I find it to be more fulfilling than I ever could have imagined." Drew is well on his way to becoming a Christ-built poet.

His name is Bob. And he is learning tenderness.

Bob, or "The Bobkins" as his wife Julie calls him, is cultivating a poet's heart. Like Drew, Bob is learning tenderness with Julie and his three children, but his great tenderness test is currently found in a smelly package named Holden.

Holden is a young man from the streets of San Francisco. Bob walked up to Holden one day while strolling downtown and said, "Hi, my name's Bob. What is your name?" Six months later, Holden's name has become a very common word in Bob's dialect.

"Holden, that is not appropriate behavior in my home."

"Holden, I don't want you saying words like that around my children."

"Holden, our bushes are for decoration not for use as your personal bathroom."

These admonitions are, of course, said very politely and with great affection.

Many times Bob has pondered how much easier life would be if he hadn't approached Holden that day. But at the same time, he's treasuring the opportunity to share the spice of tenderness with this needy man.

Bob is learning to view Holden as royalty. When he sees Holden as valuable to his King, it becomes easier to serve him and clean up after him. As Bob says, "When I serve Holden, I envision myself serving Jesus. And there is no greater privilege than that!"

Bob is also learning to become a student of Holden. He listens to Holden and validates his thoughts, fears, dreams, and desires. By understanding him, Bob's learning how to better love and serve him.

Holden is coming to Bob's church next Sunday. Holden

still struggles with the concept of taking showers, and he still isn't quite groomed for social situations. Bob's next task will be to help teach Cascade Evangelical Free Church the art of tenderness. Bob says, "I'm hoping that they embrace him as an angel sent to them from heaven—and I also hope he doesn't go to the bathroom in the bushes outside the church." Though Holden has added his share of stress to Bob's life, he has also brought a tremendous blessing—an amazing practice ground for true tenderness. Bob is well on his way to becoming a Christ-built poet.

His name is Turner. And he is learning tenderness.

Turner is a twenty-three-year-old man in search of a job and a wife—not necessarily in that order. Turner views this period of his life as "the cement season." As he says, "The way I build my life now will be the foundation for the rest of my days on this earth." Turner has discovered Jesus Christ in a whole new way these past couple years. He says, "I always knew about God, but now He's really *real* to me!"

Turner has always known that Jesus Christ was divine royalty, but now he's learning to live in accordance with that reality. Just the other day Turner said, "When you realize how holy and how powerful He is, it changes the way you approach Him. I cherish every moment the King of kings allows me to share in His amazing presence. I come to Him first thing every morning and say, 'How can I serve you today, my great King?'"

The most exciting thing about what Turner is doing is that He is learning to observe his King, study his King, and listen to his King. He desires to know the heart and mind of his King so he can more effectively love and serve Him. He is learning tenderness in his love relationship with Christ. And just as a husband studies the contours of his wife's body and learns to cherish her every thought, so Turner is learning to understand the contours of His King's heart and to cherish His every Word.

As Turner learns to put the needs, feelings, and desires of his King ahead of his own, he is preparing himself to be a world-class husband and a true Christ-built poet.

The Spice of Affection

Men are taught to see emotions as a yippy poodle with a big bow on its head—like yippy poodles, emotions draw way too much attention and look way too froufrou for a tough guy to be lugging around.

I'm a very different man today than I was fourteen years ago in high school. As my mom says, I'm "not a stiff board anymore." In fact, I've become a fairly good cuddler for Leslie. Hugs are now very natural for me. In fact, every once in a while I give a great big hug to a member of the Brotherhood and chuckle to myself when he gives me the "stiff board" hug in return.

My heart has been softened, and therefore my exterior has dramatically softened, too. I don't cry very often, but I *can* cry now. In fact, my brother and I spent so many years *unable* to cry that we now give each other high fives whenever we find an opportunity to feel emotion at that level. I love to be moved to emotion and sense the stirrings of God within my soul. And I love to express affection.

The word *affection* has been lumped in with dresses, panty hose, and eyeliner, and is therefore off-limits to any man hoping to be respectable in the modern world. But a man without affection is like a tongue without taste buds. A mouth and tongue can function without a sense of taste, but their ability is merely mechanical. There is no joy in eating, no delight in *experiencing* food.

Similarly, men can still function nobly and kindly without affection, but we do so as an outflow of *duty* rather than *desire*. Affection is the taste bud of the heart; it is the stringed instrument of the soul. When our manly souls are possessed by the Life of our King, He plays upon our heart strings the way a master violinist plays upon a Stradivarius. He moves us to feel what He feels. He stirs us to long for what He longs for. And He ignites our hearts with the same fire that burns within His own.

God-inspired emotions add a rousing movie score to the background of our life, a riot of brilliant color to our perspective, and the rich fragrance of passion to our every movement on this earth. We must realize that emotion isn't a yippy poodle; it is a Christ-directed orchestra within a true man's heart.

I have come a long way from my days of awkwardly giggling during heart-rending movies. There have since been moments in my life when I have felt so deeply that I wept from pure euphoria. I remember kneeling before Leslie and asking her to be my wife. In that moment I felt the grass of heaven beneath me and the crystal blue sky of paradise above me. I was surrounded with an angelic choir, with the scent of a million fragrant lilies in my soul.

At other times I have burned with the fiery white light of anger when I've seen the deliberate perversion of God's Truth. The jealousy of my King flushed my cheeks, and the flame of God roared within my soul.

There have even been moments of the most placid satisfaction—moments when all my cares vanished before the gargantuan presence of my Almighty King. My soul danced with the pure pleasure of freedom and the complete and utter sense of fulfillment and hope.

I have felt the stinging pain of compassion stab at my heart. I have felt the rousing ovation of joy cheer within my being. I have felt the vacuum of aloneness pull at my soul until I finally allowed it to throw me, desperate of friendship, into the waiting and open arms of my King. My King has unlocked the passions of my soul, and I would never dream of going back to my days of being a "stiff board" with a machine for a heart.

Affection is not for the delicate or faint of heart. It's for those ready to wrangle the longhorns of life, scale walls of impossibility, and venture into caves of the blackest black. The wimp shies away from expressing affection; but the *true man*, the warrior poet, embraces it in all its pain and promise.

As young men, we must beware of Self's counterfeit version of affection. If Self controls our soul, Self controls our heart. Self produces *perverted* emotions that starve our covenant Life rather than feed it. When Self produces the emotion of love, it becomes a self-serving and lustful thing. If Self produces anger, it becomes a Self-defending and violent rage. If Self seeks happiness, its pleasure is conditional, dependent upon Self-success and Self-comfort.

> The true man, the warrior poet, embraces affection in all its pain and promise.

To truly connect with the emotional matrix of our King, we must submit our heart fully to Him. Then we will love from a *selfless* heart, become angry from a *selfless* longing for Truth, and discover that our covenant Life with our King is our true source of pure happiness. The presence of godly affection will transform a man from a *parrot* of truth into a *poet* of truth.

✎

His name is Cal. And he is learning to show affection.

After years of life as a heartless machine, Cal is feeling emotion course through his soul for the first time. His wife, Adriane, doesn't know quite what to do with her new Cal. She says, "It's like the thawing of Ice Man!"

Cal was raised by the Brotherhood and, therefore, taught not to feel emotion except when it came to sex, sports, and spicy-hot salsa. But then, Cal says, "I asked God to allow me to begin feeling what He feels." With a wry grin he adds, "I guess He took me up on it."

Cal is developing the habit of asking God, whenever he meets someone, what God's thoughts are toward that person and what He feels when He sees them. If God is concerned for them, Cal becomes concerned. If God is happy, Cal becomes happy. And if God is feeling pain, Cal is learning to feel the burden of someone else's pain. "It's still easy for me to hole up in my Self-built cave," Cal admits, "but I'm getting more and more aware of the needs of those around me. When you haven't felt true emotion for twenty-five years, it's kind of a strange rush."

I am inspired by another of Cal's new spiritual habits. He calls it his "temple whippings" behavior pattern, referring to the instance when Jesus grabbed a whip and went full throttle into an emotional tirade when he saw people turning the temple of God into a marketplace. Cal says, "I'm not the kind of guy that gets upset easily. Terrible things can happen around me, and I can easily remain unfazed." He smiles. "That is, *until now!*"

Whenever Cal spots injustice, twisting of truth, or callous behavior toward the weak, he asks God what His feelings are toward those evils. If God is incensed, Cal is incensed. If God is saddened, then Cal is learning to be saddened, too.

Cal's relationship with Christ is becoming more emotional as well. Jesus had always existed as a calculated and important truth to Cal, but He was never a real person. Now Cal is learning to cultivate a romance with his King. He's listening to His voice, talking to Him throughout the day, walking with Him, sharing every moment at His side.

Sometimes he simply stares into His glorious face. Cal says, "I finally understand what it means to love Him from both the mind *and* the heart."

⌒

Affection is a lost art in the modern realm of masculinity. It's as rare as the dodo bird and just about as strange to a man's mind. But affection is critical to the full and complete formation of a Christ-built poet. The spice of affection is as important to a man's heart as salt is to a bowl of popcorn—a man can't taste the brilliant beauty of God's creation without it.

A poet's heart is the spring from which the Life of God bubbles and flows into this world. It's a heart seasoned with the tender grace of the King and salted with His passionate affection. For a man to accurately share the gospel message with this world, his heart must first have been captured and cultivated by the divine power of Love.

"Do nothing from selfishness or conceit,
but in humility count others better than yourselves.
Let each of you look not only to his own interests,
but also to the interests of others."[24]
PAUL THE APOSTLE

"I will take away their hearts of stone
and give them tender hearts instead."[25]
GOD THE FATHER

12

The Pursuit

Following in the Steps of Our Prince

ou've got to read it, Eric," my brother-in-law David pronounced. "It is the single greatest book I have ever read."

"I just don't have time," I retorted. "I have so many other books I'm trying to get through."

"You need to make time for it," Leslie's dad, Rich, said. "It is a spectacular story."

With great emotion and profound conviction, David and Rich sang the praises of the greatest book they had both ever read. *The Sienkiewicz Triology* had moved them so deeply that they now longed for others to be stirred in the very same way. They had tasted something that they knew others just had to taste.

"What did you say this book is about?" I asked with a doubtful expression plastered across my face.

"It's about the crisis facing Poland in the sixteenth century," David offered, "but it's an amazing story!"

Yeah right! I thought. How could a crisis facing Poland in the sixteenth century possibly be of interest to me? The book—divided into four massive volumes—was four thousand pages in length. What a terrible bore!

It took them about a month of persuasion before I finally cracked open the first of the four volumes. Sometimes a book that looks boring and difficult can, if truly experienced, come to life and carry you away on wings of pure delight. *The Sienkiewicz Trilogy* is definitely in that category.

From that point forward, every chance I could I crept away to a quiet spot and read. It was a magical journey, stirring within me laughter, tears, anger, and pure unadulterated delight. It's a masterpiece of the most epic proportions.

When I finished the book, I became its greatest champion. I took up its cause and crusaded for everyone I knew to read it. Every one of my family members received four volumes of great literature for Christmas that year. When I spoke to groups about guy/girl relationships, I would invariably mention this amazing story as a must-read for everyone in my audience, ignoring the fact that sixteenth century Poland didn't remotely relate to my topic of romance. I would spend a good five minutes persuading everyone to find this book and read it and that they would regret it forever if they did not.

Too many of us hear about great books and never read them, the same way we hear about Jesus Christ and never really *know* Him. The idea of knowing Christ can sound like reading four thousand pages about sixteenth century Poland.

But in actuality, to know Christ is to be carried away by a life-absorbing Love on the wings of pure delight.

Like discovering a great piece of literature, once we crack open the Life of Christ and begin to read Him, understand Him, and know Him, we just can't put Him down. Every spare moment we desire to share life at His side, following Him, listening to Him, loving Him. And when we experience Him, we have to share Him with others. We just can't keep it in. The beauty and brilliance that we found in our King we now desire everyone to experience and know.

The amazing thing about reading the life-changing literature called Jesus Christ is the story never ends. There is always more to discover, more adventures to share, and more tales to tell. He's like a great book that can be savored for all eternity.

A poet's heart hungers for more. He's not satisfied with exploring only the west coast of God's great continent of Truth. A poet hungers to explore it all, region by region, state by state, county by county, city by city, home by home, closet by closet, and shoebox by shoebox. A Christ-built poet has an insatiable thirst for Christ. He wants to know His mind, His heart, His pain, His delight, His concerns, and His desires. A true poet can't just hear about the book; a true poet must read it for himself. A true poet isn't satisfied with merely being told that God is good; he must *taste and see* that He is good.[26]

> Too many of us hear about Jesus Christ but never really know Him.

So how can we, as poets, pursue our great Heavenly

Lover? Let's look at how we can cultivate an even deeper relationship with our King and learn to think what He thinks, feel what He feels, go where He goes, and do what He does.

The Poet's Pursuit

If we desired to *really* know and understand a homeless man, we would spend time with him on the streets. We would dress like him, allow ourselves to be treated like him, and even sleep under a bridge beside him. By going where he goes and doing what he does, we would probably form a special bond with him. We would share in his sufferings, and therefore know his heart by feeling what he feels.

To know Christ is very much the same. We must go where He goes and do what He does. We must learn to Love the way He does, be treated like He was treated here on earth, and even feel the sting of loneliness the way He felt it. Because in so doing, we will form a special bond of intimate understanding with our King.

A Christ-built poet must combine a poet's heart with a poet's pursuit. The poet's pursuit is to be where Christ is and to share in what Christ is doing. But Christ isn't always found in clean-smelling church buildings. He is often found under bridges sleeping next to the homeless man, mowing the overgrown lawn of a lonely widow, or gently stroking the cheek of a crying orphan. The poet's heart feels what Christ feels, but the poet's pursuit leads him to go where Christ would go and do what Christ would do. The poet's pursuit is a path of sacrifice.

The Spice of Sacrifice

Sacrifice is a mind-set. Much like tenderness, it is a daily decision to serve the King's Life and interests rather than serve Self's life and interests. I took some of my first steps of sacrifice working as a missionary in inner city New Orleans in the autumn of 1992. My opportunity to serve my King came in the smelly package of Myron, a urine-stained homeless guy.

I grew up in a family that prized personal hygiene. We brushed our teeth a minimum of twice a day, showered or bathed often, and rotated our clothing to avoid the "That's disgusting!" effect. Even though my mom every once in a while had to remind me to replace my ratty boxers or gargle with high-powered mouthwash, for the most part I was a clean guy. Most days I smelled of my fresh-scented deodorant with just a hint of Downey fabric softener.

To put it mildly, Myron subscribed to a different version of hygiene. His scent was more a blend of an armpit smell after two years of caked-up sweat and the pungent odor of a Port-a-Jon on a hot July afternoon. The first time I came within five feet of him, I nearly keeled over with a hemorrhage of the nasal passage. Yet I was reminded that God cared about Myron, and I knew it was Myron that God asked me to serve.

Myron was staying in the halfway house next door, and I knew he would be stopping by the next day. So I went to work on "Operation Myron." I didn't have a clear-cut vision for what this mission was supposed to be. All I knew was that my King loved this smelly man and He wanted me to express His love to Myron in a practical way. I didn't have any money, so I had to be creative. I teamed up with another young missionary student named Stacy. We wrapped some presents for Myron and set them on the counter where he always stirred his coffee. I had picked out my favorite sweatshirt as the ideal gift for Myron. My King was gently challenging me, "My son, I gave My best for you. Can you give your best back to Me?" So my gift to Myron was the best item of clothing I owned— my red Nike sweatshirt fit me perfectly and was the one item in my closet I always knew would come through for me. Stacy wrapped up her prized Walkman CD player. We tied ribbon around our packages and put a note on top that said simply, "Myron."

I'll never forget the moment Myron first laid eyes on the two packages. While he stirred his coffee, he looked down and saw the note that read "Myron." He just kept stirring his coffee. After another few minutes passed and Myron had finished his daily cup-o-caffeine, I meandered into the kitchen to help Myron along.

"Hey, Myron!" I greeted him cheerfully.

Myron didn't say a word. In fact, I don't know that I had ever heard Myron say a word. He simply looked away as if perturbed by my presence.

"What's this?" I said with a hint of surprise in my voice. "Are these packages for you?"

"No!" Myron grunted, uttering words for the first time since I'd met him.

"Don't they say 'Myron' on them?" I countered with brilliant logic.

Myron paused and stared down at the packages. And then again looked away in disinterest, acting as if he were going to pour another cup of coffee.

"Myron," I said, realizing I was going to have to be a little more direct, "these presents are for *you!*"

Myron sat silent for a long time staring at his coffee cup. I fidgeted with a pile of mail, as if this whole scene didn't affect me. I desperately wanted Myron to be touched by this sacrifice of mine. My heart raced as Myron finally reached out toward the packages and plucked the note off the top. He opened it. It read, "Myron, this is just a reminder that you are loved and appreciated. Enjoy the gifts."

After reading the note again five or six times, he finally set it down and slowly reached for the two packages. Stacy was watching discreetly from the hall, and I kept glancing over from the far side of the kitchen as I made a peanut butter and jelly sandwich.

Fifteen minutes later, Myron was clothed in my cherished red Nike sweatshirt and wearing Stacy's headphones. He sat down in a La-Z-Boy chair in the living room of our missionary house. His pants were wet with urine, and his smell permeated the entire room; but at that moment I didn't care about the future of the chair or about the future of my ability to smell. I was flooded with compassion for my new friend, Myron. I sat next to him in a kitchen chair that I had pulled in from the other room and tried to talk with him.

"Are you enjoying your Walkman?" I asked. When he didn't respond, I tried another tact. "You look great in that red sweatshirt!" But there was still nothing audible from the smelly, comatose Myron.

I sat there with him for some time, saying nothing, but trying to love him with my presence. I came close to gagging quite a few times, but after ten minutes, I started to adjust to the awful stench. It was strange and awkward, but I silently put my arm around his shoulder and just held it there.

Soon, tears began to fill his eyes. He sniffled a little and continued to stare straight ahead with the headphones on, even though the batteries to the Walkman were still in his hand.

Then after another few minutes, he huskily spoke.

"No one's ever given me a gift before." With that, he choked and swallowed hard and then repeated his statement as if he desired it to be italicized, *"No one's ever given me a gift before."*

Sacrificing my precious red Nike sweatshirt for Myron was just a baby step in my journey as a Christ-built poet. But it was huge in my development as a man. It is those first steps of obedience that train us in the extraordinary internal reward of forgetting our Self and treasuring Christ. It is those baby steps of obedience that prove to our souls the inestimable value of willingly sacrificing when our King requests. The spice of sacrifice is a powerful life-altering gift to both the receiver *and* the giver.

From the outside, it would appear that a life of sacrifice is a life of discomfort and pain. But actually, a life of sacrifice is a life of matchless satisfaction and exhilaration. To go where our King goes and do what our King is doing is to forge a deep and eternal friendship with the God of the universe.

The Spice of Desire

To know God is to love Him. It is impossible to encounter the tender grace of our King and not find limitless satisfaction in His goodness and mercy. To encounter God is to taste the sweetest most scrumptious delights of the soul.

"You take this Christianity thing way too seriously!" muttered a longtime friend of mine. "You are wasting your perfectly good human life."

Describing the beauties of knowing Christ to someone who has never tasted them is like trying to describe the sound of a banjo to a person deaf since birth. The only people who will say it is a waste of a life to pursue more and more of Jesus Christ are those who have never met Him.

As humans, we are changed by personally experiencing the beautiful things of life. And so we follow our passions, we train to explore them deeper, and we surround ourselves with that which we love. How much more should that be true about us as Christ-built men? Christ-built poets have discovered the splendor and grandeur of their Almighty King and felt His very Life course through their veins. Their entire life is now ruined for an average existence. They now wake up each morning eager to pursue more of their King. They train to explore Him deeper, and they surround themselves with His very presence.

Men spend months, often years, of their life devoted to the passionate pursuit of their desires. Hunting, athletics, computers, cars, music—men will spend both their time and money to follow their passion to its fullest. Some go to college and study it. Some shoot baskets every night to become it. Some jack up machines in their garages so they can explore it. God designed men to have desire and to passionately pursue their interests. But God intended that man's great pursuit would begin with a passionate longing to know and understand Him.

What would our manhood be like if we pursued Christ the way we have been trained to pursue the opposite sex? What would our manhood be like if we spent the same amount of time chasing down Truth as we do tinkering with our computers, cars, athletic skills, musical talents, or hunting rifles?

The Pursuit of Intimacy

To know our God, to feel what He feels, to go where He goes, and to do what He does, requires that we become His eager students. We must enter the School of Christ. And the core curriculum in the School of Christ is designed to hone and develop five "pursuit" abilities that enable a man to feed the Life within his soul. Each of these five abilities deserve an entire book of their own. My purpose for mentioning them here is to awaken you to their importance. It is left up to you to pursue and cultivate their life-altering power.

Stillness

Stillness is the art of calibrating our pace to match God's pace instead of the world's pace. This culture around us is moving at a frenetic speed, always in a hurry and always concerned with keeping up with the fast lane. Meanwhile, God moves slowly, growing up His Life within the souls of His poets, teaching them to lean completely on Him, to trust Him to take care of their every need, and depend on Him for every little thing the future holds. Those who cultivate the covenant Life share in the glorious peace and unruffled nature of the Life of God. They share in His confidence, His placid demeanor, and His quiet assurance of victory.

I read that Hudson Taylor, the great Christian missionary to China, learned the unruffled Life of Christ to the point where the internal environment of his soul was constant and unwavering. Nothing could thwart his trusting attitude toward his God. He could receive a pile of mail, including bills that he didn't have money to pay, a telegram announcing the death of a friend in the mission field, as well as perplexing news from family back home, and read them all with the same stillness of heart and mind. He learned to constantly lean on the trustworthiness of his King, knowing that His God was always in complete control.

Every time I pick up my mail or read my e-mail, I think of Hudson Taylor. When I receive the unexpected blows, devastating news, and unsolvable riddles of life, I'm learning to immediately turn to my King and whisper, "I trust You!" Stillness is the soil in which the covenant Life grows. It's the waters in which the perfect reflection of the heavens can be seen. It is the foundation stone of the other four arts of intimacy.[27]

Biblical Study

The Life of God within our souls needs food. For it to grow and be healthy it needs to eat. While our human bodies may subsist on a diet of cheeseburgers and potato salad, the diet of the covenant Life is quite different—it feeds on *the truths of Scripture*.

To read the Bible is a beginning, but more importantly, we need to study and understand it. Our King desires us to know Him, and the chief way He has provided for us to do that is to understand Him through Scripture. The Bible is the expression of God's heart, the thoughts of God's mind, and the feelings of God's soul. The Bible explains the covenant Life, it helps train us in the covenant Life, and cheers us on in the covenant Life.

The art of Biblical study involves learning how to observe the Scripture and unravel its many layers of beauty and troll its infinite depths. It involves learning to correctly handle the Truth and properly interpret its meaning. And it involves learning to rightly apply it to our lives, so that we don't just know *about* truth but we live it out, in vibrant color, for the entire world to see.

Biblical Meditation

To meditate on something means to touch it, taste it, smell it, and feel it with the mind and heart. Biblical meditation is an art form meant to stir the affection of a Christian. It's a personal encounter with the beauty of God. It's tasting His delectable love with our heart. It's smelling His awe-inspiring cologne with the nostrils of our mind and feeling the grandeur of His nature with the fingertips of our soul.

Biblical meditation is a discipline of passion. It's the focusing of our energies into the pure enjoyment of our God—thinking about His awesome traits, reflecting on His great love, pondering and imagining how much greater God is than what we can even conceive today.

Christians throughout history have used Biblical meditation to prepare their hearts for worshiping their King. Meditation is allowing the Spirit of God within to unlock the beauty of Jesus Christ for our mind and our heart. When we encounter face to face the glory of our King, we fall to our knees in worshipful abandon and cry out, "You are wonderful. You are holy. You are perfect, my precious Jesus!" Meditation on Christ equals heartfelt worship of Christ.

Worship

Worship isn't merely singing to God. Though worship can be expressed through singing, it is far more than mere musical expression. Worship is the adoration of the soul. Worship is the reverent expression of a burning heart. Worship is a result of meditation on Christ, a result of seeing the reality of Christ's greatness in Scripture. It is the natural reaction of a soul enjoying the Life of God.

Worship is heartfelt delight in the person of Christ. It's telling Him, whether through a love song, a love letter, or a life of love lived, that He is the essence of everything we know and love. Heartfelt worship is an attitude maintained and directed toward every moment of every day. We can let our God know with every movement of our body, every thought in our mind, and every feeling of our heart that He is the exhilarating love of our life.

Prayer

Prayer is nothing more than talking with God. It doesn't demand audible sound; it can be talking with the mind or as simple as yearning with the heart. God is an interpreter of even our moaning and longings. Prayer is the means by which God allows us to share the adventures of life with Him. Prayer is the connection, the spiritual rope that binds our heart and mind with our King's every moment of the day.

Prayer is continually acknowledging His presence as He walks with us down the sidewalk, as He sits down beside us at lunch, and as He watches by our side when we lay our head down on our pillow at night. He shares our every moment, and prayer is *grabbing hold of that reality* and using it to build the covenant Life.

Prayer is sometimes an utterance of the heart, such as "God, give me wisdom for this decision." Sometimes prayer is turning the eyes of our soul His way and yielding to His desire, as in "What do You want me to do in this situation?" Sometimes prayer is a plea for someone else, such as "Please help my friend to see the reality of You!" And sometimes prayer is nothing more than sharing moments of silence throughout our day with our King—not saying a word, but simply cherishing His goodness.

Each of these five arts of intimacy takes a lifetime, possibly even an eternity, to master. But the covenant Life grows within us as we cultivate and develop these arts of intimacy. To know God, we must become students of Him. Let's sign up for the School of Christ and begin our endless pursuit of the great and mighty God of the universe.

It is sometimes easy for us to compare our spiritual lives to Christians around us and settle where they choose to settle. Modern-day Christians often pay their dues by attending church once or twice a week and reading their Bibles for five minutes every now and then. Let's not pitch our tents in the realm of the norm. Knowing our King is an endless frontier of discovery, passion, and depth. To pursue Him with all our heart, soul, mind, and strength is to experience the fullness of joy.

Eric Ludy

"Not that I have already obtained this or am already perfect;
but I press on to make it my own,
because Christ Jesus has made me his own.
Brethren, I do not consider that I have made it my own;
but one thing I do, forgetting what lies behind
and straining forward to what lies ahead,
I press on toward the goal for the prize of the
upward call of God in Christ Jesus."28

PAUL THE APOSTLE

13

The Poetic Lover
Becoming Excellent in Intimate Love

early every guy I've ever met would love to know the secret of satisfying a woman sexually. Most guys think that the secret of success in romantic love lies in great kissing technique or giving off sexy Tom Cruise vibes. But the secret to satisfying a woman has very little to do with our ability to give smoldering looks or passionate kisses. To become excellent in intimate love we must be excellent at relational *intimacy*. This is ironic, because if there is one thing that sounds even more cloudlike and fluffy to a guy than the word *tenderness*, it is the word *intimacy*.

"What does intimacy mean to you?" I polled a group of single guys recently during a male-only coffee shop chat.

"Dude, why do we have to talk about something like that?" came the blustery protest from around the table. The guys would have much rather talked about sex, or at the very least, girls. Intimacy was the last thing on their list of preferred topics. Yet intimacy is usually the *first thing* on a woman's list of desires. When we cultivate intimacy with our spouse, she naturally gives herself completely and fully to us emotionally and physically. If you want great sex in your future marriage, begin laying the foundation for great intimacy now.

As Christ-built warriors, we learn to valiantly protect a woman's heart. As Christ-built poets, we learn to nobly *cherish* a woman's heart by nurturing Christ-centered intimacy. Intimacy is something that we can prepare for, even before we meet our future spouse.

"But what in the world *is* intimacy?" wonders a generation of guys, who are about as clear on the concept as a baboon is on international politics.

Guys today don't understand intimacy because, for the most part, we have never seen it. Many of our dads grunt at our mothers from behind a newspaper, selfishly indulge in affairs or pornography, or have simply checked out altogether. Even many of the more solid marriages among the older generation seem sadly lacking in beauty and sparkle. But our King desires so much more for us when it comes to earthly romance, and it starts with us as Christ-built men. We must set a new standard for our future marriages by learning the secrets of the Christ-built lover.

The Core of True Intimacy

Intimacy at its very root is private. It's the secret sharing of life and love. Intimacy wouldn't be intimacy if you told your buddies every "sweet nothing" you had whispered into your lover's ear the night before. For intimacy to retain its luster and brilliance, it must be kept guarded and barricaded in the citadel of secrecy.

If we as young men are to ever discover the heavenly glories of intimacy, we must become excellent secret-holders. The secrets of intimacy aren't the type of secrets that make for good espionage thrillers; they're the kind of secrets that expose the vulnerability of the heart.

I have entrusted Leslie with countless secrets of this kind over the years.

"Leslie, I look like an idiot when I go swing dancing."

"Leslie, I am afraid of actually putting my head under the water."

"Leslie, I really want you to come watch me play basketball tonight."

"Leslie, I feel like you deserve better than me for a husband."

I have many more secrets, but Leslie would never tell them to you. In fact, intimacy thrives in our marriage because Leslie would never consider sharing the secret vulnerabilities of my soul with the world around her. And I guard her secrets, too, as I would my most prized possessions. Our secrets are fuel for intimacy. Intimacy is the purest form of feeling loved and cherished, because it's feeling loved and cherished while being spiritually, emotionally, and/or physically naked in front of your lover.

A Christ-built poet knows when to speak to a woman in

a whisper and when not to speak at all. He knows the difference between a sexual touch and an affirming touch, and he is an expert on knowing exactly when the appropriate power of touch should be gently employed. A Christ-built poet knows how to yield to the needs of a woman's heart and not to his own hormonal impulses.

We must learn to focus on *giving to our wife* emotionally and physically rather than *receiving from her* emotionally and physically. A true poet learns to artistically express his love in ways that make a woman feel cherished and adored. We must become students of our lover's femininity, knowing just the right moments to encourage her with a love note, cheer her with a dinner out, or surprise her with a thoughtfully chosen flower. A Christ-built poet, when polished by the gentle hand of God, is the single most powerful visible and physical representation of Christ's love to womanhood. A true poet is truly a gift to femininity.

Modern guys train to excel in sports, business, even beer drinking; but rarely, if ever, do we train to be excellent in marriage. Olympic athletes practice six hours a day for years to show the world that they are the greatest at their event. What if young men were to train at a world-class level to be outrageously good at protecting and serving femininity?

> The Christ-built poet yields to the needs of a woman's heart and not to his own hormonal impulses.

What would happen if we, as young men, started spending our energies honing our character and cultivating our covenant Life rather than burping the alphabet and picking lint from our belly buttons?

A great marriage is a result of great intimacy, and great intimacy is achieved as the result of strenuous Olympic-like training. If you are serious about becoming an excellent husband someday, start cultivating the following five abilities today.

1. The Ability to Truly Listen

We've all been in a conversation with someone who wasn't listening. I told a guy the other day on the phone that Leslie and I were going to be in his neck of the woods soon and would love to get together with him. He was distractedly silent for a couple seconds and then, realizing it was his turn to talk, suddenly laughed and said, "Yeah! That's hilarious!"

Growing up, we are taught techniques for almost every form of communication in school, from writing to speaking to finger painting. But the ability to truly listen, while it may be the most important communication skill a human can develop, is almost completely overlooked. Volumes are spoken when you effectively listen to someone. Listening says, "You are important to me. I want to understand you better. What you have to say matters."

I can't state enough how important this ability is in a marriage. If Leslie starts talking to me and senses that I'm not listening, she will stop and not say another word. In fact, if she shares an intimate secret with me and I'm thinking about the Broncos game, any intimate connection between us shuts down immediately.

"Did you hear what I just said?" Leslie says.

"Of course I heard you," I'll respond, hoping she doesn't ask me to repeat her words back.

"Well then, what did I say?" she tests me with a slanted eyebrow.

"Uh," I stumble, "you were talking about some deep things. Why don't you continue?" As brilliant as this come-back is, Leslie never falls for it. She always seems to know when I'm not connected. And since I deeply value our intimacy, I work really hard to be connected whenever she talks to me. When I don't listen to Leslie, she interprets it as me saying, "I have something more important to ponder than your thoughts and feelings." But when I do listen, it opens up a floodgate of dazzling intimacy between us.

When Leslie talks to me, I've learned to let her know I'm listening by making little agreement noises when she's talking. I shake my head to let her know I understand, and I laugh when she says something funny. One of the most powerful listening techniques I've learned is repeating back in my own words what it is I think I'm hearing her say to me. When Leslie feels listened to and understood, she feels secure and cherished as my wife.

Even before you are married, you can practice the art of listening. After you are married you will still be perfecting the ability, so why not get a head start by becoming great at it now? Life is your practice ground—you can refine this ability every day in every conversation. True intimacy, whether spiritual or marital, hinges upon your ability to truly listen.

2. The Ability to Be Tender

We have already discussed the importance and power of tenderness, but since it is a critical component of intimacy in a relationship, let's look at how we can specifically prepare to be tender poets for our brides-to-be.

There is no better (and no safer) training ground for tenderness than mothers and sisters. Since tenderness, when applied rightly, is a super-potent tool for warming a woman's affections, it is crucial that a young man learn this ability in the safe confines of his home rather than on every young woman who crosses his path. We so often overlook the members of our own family—we assume that their feelings and thoughts are less valuable simply because they are related to us. But if we can learn to excel at demonstrating tenderness toward our moms and sisters, we will be amazing at displaying tenderness with our future spouse.

For a young man to be truly tender with a woman, he must be a great observer of femininity. I don't mean an observer of the outside of a woman, but of the inner workings of her heart and mind. Tenderness, very simply defined, is giving to someone else that which they most need in the moment they most need it.

For a young man practicing tenderness with his mom and sisters it might look like this: a cup of cold water lovingly delivered to a sister on a hot summer day; an arm of support and comfort around the shoulder of a mother in a moment of tears; the words "Wow! You look beautiful!" gently spoken to a sister when she first walks into the living room on a night when she desires to look her best; or the words "Thanks for being such a wonderful mother" uttered on days other than Mother's Day.

If a young man can learn to be great at tenderness with his mother and sisters, he will become every woman's dream in marriage, and he will be unrivaled in his preparation for personal intimacy with Jesus Christ.

3. The Ability to Enjoy the Journey

This world is always in a hurry, always in a rush to arrive. We pace impatiently in front of microwaves, become irritable when the speed limit drops from seventy-five to fifty-five, and sigh in frustration when the drive-thru takes longer than two minutes. But God is never in a hurry and is never in a rush to arrive. He wants to enjoy the adventure with us along the way.

Men on road trips tend to be preoccupied with what women fondly (or not so fondly) refer to as "conquering miles." We want to get from point A to point B in record time. We refuse to acknowledge our screaming bladder for hours at a time, and our eyes glaze over with rugged determination. Meanwhile, we miss the beauty of God's creation as we race onward, meditating on the pavement, the rearview mirror, and man's favorite driving companion, *the speedometer.* And so we tend to miss the opportunities for meaningful conversation with our passengers.

Young men need to transition from conquering the miles of life to enjoying the journey and taking each moment as an opportunity to deepen our covenant Life. A man who trains himself on how to enjoy the process rather than just the arrival is a man who will be truly amazing in mastering the romantic elements of life, with both his future wife and with his Heavenly King.

Sexual intimacy is made wonderful for both husband and wife when the man learns to "enjoy the journey." So often a married man is interested in only one thing when he enters into physical intimacy with his wife—the sex act. But the sex act is only a small part of sexual intimacy. It's the destination, but it's not the entire journey.

When you get married, remember to take time with your wife in the bedroom and move at the pace of *her* heart and *her* body's arousal. I guarantee you the enjoyment factor of sex will multiply dramatically. If sexual intimacy were defined by a man's body clock, the entire act would be over and done with in less than five minutes. That is why a man must allow his wife to define the pace of awakening and enjoying romantic love. God designed the woman to be the pacesetter in the bedroom. Her sexual journey of lovemaking, from tender words and romantic touching to heated embrace and the finality of sexual climax, can last for hours.

Sexual intimacy is just one of the many reasons that before we say "I do," we need to learn to enjoy the journey and not just reach the destination.

4. The Ability to Be Thoughtful

When a young man first falls for the girl of his dreams, thoughtfulness comes rather easily. He sends flowers and writes poems expressing a love packed with roses and rhymes for all time. For a young man, when love is new, visions of his fair maiden will linger in his mind twenty-four hours a day. But when he becomes more familiar with her, when the sweet papaya fragrance that wafts from her hair no longer causes his knees to buckle, and the springtime blossom of love has faded, many men unfortunately run empty on thoughtfulness. But thoughtfulness is critical to intimacy and was never intended to be reserved only for the season of falling in love. Men must learn how to be thoughtful as a way of life.

Once again, our family is the perfect practice ground for developing thoughtfulness. In fact, anyone familiar and in close proximity, like roommates in college or irritating cousins who hang around the house, are great for thoughtfulness training. If we can learn to be thoughtful toward those we are familiar with, we will learn how to be thoughtful toward our future wife long after the honeymoon is over.

Being thoughtful simply means to give a meaningful gift or perform an act of service without being asked. Here are a few examples of how you can practice being thoughtful year-round: Buy your sister a bag of peanut M&M's (her favorite) and place them on her pillow with a note that says, "Hope your test went well"; get up early one morning and buy all your family members their favorite kind of doughnut; take your roommate's filthy Geo Metro to the car wash and fill it up with gas (on your dime); or invite your irritating little cousin to a movie with you and your buddies and buy him a popcorn and Coke. When we can learn to be thoughtful with "the roomies and the fam," we will be ready to keep the roses and rhymes alive with our future wife and live happily ever after.

People say that romance dies after the honeymoon, but those are people who stopped being thoughtful toward their spouses. Thoughtfulness was only a tool to win their spouse's heart before marriage, but they failed to cherish their spouse's heart after the "I do's" were exchanged.

Leslie loves receiving flowers and notes, but one of her favorite "thoughtful" gestures is my cleaning the house without her asking me. It may not seem like a very romantic gesture, but it works wonders for the intimacy of our marriage. We work together during the day, and every once in a while, I'll get up from my desk and sneak into her office, tenderly wrap my arms around her neck, and give her a kiss on the cheek. Thoughtfulness is made up of such little statements of love and adoration.

Remember, a thoughtful husband is a happy husband because he produces a smiling wife.

5. The Ability to Develop Spiritual Oneness

As my relationship with Leslie was unfolding, I received an invaluable piece of wisdom from my own personal Yoda—

her dad, Rich. "To experience intimacy in its fullness," he told me one day over buttermilk pancakes, "it should be built in three stages—spiritual oneness, emotional oneness, and then physical oneness in marriage. It is important not to rush to the next stage until the previous one has been thoroughly established."

Many Christian guys begin relationships with the confident declaration, "We are building this relationship with Jesus Christ at the center!" But after a few weeks or months, they are often swimming in an unpredictable sea of raging emotions and physical temptation. Keeping Jesus Christ at the core of a relationship is much easier said than done. Physical attraction can get in the way, blinding us to everything but our own intense longing to be with the other person. Sexual desire can get in the way, flooding us with insatiable longings to express our passion for the other person physically. Soon, the relationship we thought was centered on our King becomes nothing more than a physical and emotional roller-coaster ride that clouds everything else in life. Once a relationship is based on an emotional or physical core, it is very difficult (if not impossible) to go back and create a solid spiritual foundation. That is why the beginning stages of a relationship are absolutely crucial.

One of the best ways to develop spiritual oneness at the core of a relationship is to first savor a season of Christ-centered friendship before anything else happens. Leslie and I wanted to lay the foundation for spiritual intimacy long before emotional or physical intimacy came into the picture.

It may sound unromantic, but it was actually one of the most incredible and exciting times in our love story.

When we were together, instead of dwelling on emotional passion or physical desire for the other person, we spent our time discussing new truths we were learning in our spiritual lives. We read inspiring Christian biographies together and talked about how they impacted us. We read Scripture together and spent hours praying and thinking about how God's truth should affect our daily lives. We dreamed about ministering together and talked about ways that God might use our lives in the future. We worshiped our King together around the piano. As a team, we developed the same spiritual convictions about how to live and act and think. As time went by, though we each continued to have a strong individual relationship with our King, we also began to have a mutual relationship with Him as a couple. Jesus Christ remained at the center of our love story.

Later, when we sensed it was the right time for our emotional oneness to begin to develop, we were aware of the solid foundation of spiritual unity at the core of our relationship. Even today in our marriage, emotional and physical oneness are simply an added bonus—not the basis of our love story. Though emotional and physical desire can easily rush up and then come plunging down like a roller-coaster, a relationship built on Jesus Christ remains steady, strong, and unshakable. Both emotional and physical oneness can be experienced in their most beautiful form when spiritual oneness comes first.

As men, we desire to be incredible lovers. We desire our girl to flush with delight whenever she considers the fact that, out of all the millions of men on the planet, she has *us* for her husband. But great husbands aren't born overnight. They aren't made by mixing a few manly ingredients together in a pan and baking it for twenty minutes at four hundred degrees. It takes years of focused training, studying our King, following our King, and cultivating His Life within us. But the results are divine. In fact, a Christ-built lover is a miracle of the most epic proportion—he is a miniature replica of the great Poetic Lover Himself, Jesus Christ.

"Husbands, live considerately with your wives."[29]
PETER THE APOSTLE

"If I then, your Lord and Teacher, have washed your feet,
you also ought to wash one another's feet.
For I have given you an example,
that you also should do as I have done to you."[30]
JESUS CHRIST

Final Thoughts

o love a woman well is the epitome of great manhood. But to be capable of loving a woman well, we men must first learn to love Christ well. As men, we are called to protect and serve, but what we choose to protect and serve defines the substance of our manhood. Are you a Self-protecting and Self-serving male, heavy on the cologne and light on the character? Or are you a Truth-protecting and Christ-serving warrior poet set to positively change the world in which we live? A man protecting and serving his Self is a man empty of all that is truly noble and honorable in heaven. But a man protecting and serving the covenant Life of his King within his soul is a man exhibiting the nobility and honor of heaven itself.

Today's young men don't need another sermon. We don't need another word of advice. We don't need another book telling us what we, as men, should be. *We need the Life of our King.* And we need His Life to consume our own. We need

Him to possess our souls and own our bodies. Manhood will never change through grit and hard work. It won't better itself through reading and study. It will only become the triumph that God designed it to be by coming under the rulership of its Creator and walking in the footsteps of the heroic Lamb of God.

Manhood doesn't need a key; it needs its King.

I am only thirty-two years old. And the message in this book is still being forged into my youthful soul. My adventure into the endless frontiers of God's grace has just begun, and my manhood is still very young. I have testings ahead that will try the metal of my soul. In the days to come I will face sufferings that will draw out and purge the dross of remaining immaturity. I don't expect my life to be easy. In fact, I expect my life to be full of the challenges that come with standing against the tide. And I am willing to stand alone. But I would love to have you standing with me. I would love to know that there are other young men out there with a similar hunger for Christ, for His Truth, and for His Life.

The message of this book is simple: Manhood that is truly great is manhood built by God. Everything else is but a creative counterfeit of the original. As a young man, I'm tired of the counterfeits and I'm longing for the authentic version. I ache to have a Hero, sagacious in the Spirit of God, thunderously implore me to stand up and be counted as a man. There is something inside me that yearns to have a William Wallace grasp me by the arm and heroically breathe into my ear, "All men die, but few men ever live! Ludy, follow me!" I want to follow a great and mighty Christ-built man. I want to learn from a Gandalf-like leader. But I must also be willing to _become_ that leader. I must allow God to forge me into a man like William Wallace. And you must allow God to do the same with you.

We can pray for great men to lead us, but are we willing to be the answer to that prayer and become the men that lead? Are we willing to be the first to die, to spark the revolution? Are we willing to be the first to speak, to spark the reformation? Are we willing to be the first to stand, to spark the reclamation of the gospel?

We, as young men, need just one of our peers to stand up and trust his God completely without reserve. We need just one who will brave the winds of loneliness and scorn and start climbing the rugged mountain cliffs in the direction of his King. We need just one to hear the call of the wild and charge the fields of Bannockburn to fight for something that really matters. We need just one to stand, and manhood in this modern culture could be forever altered. Will you be that one?

I ask you to take this battle seriously. I ask you to embrace the painful prick of conviction that stings your heart. I ask you to find a quiet place and get alone with your King. I ask you to consider presenting your life to Him, for Him to do with as He sees fit. I promise you the battle will be fierce. But one thing I can assure you: If you lean the weight of your life on His strong and sovereign chest, He will make you into a great man, and He will never leave your side. He will forge you into a protector of the covenant Life, and He will shape you into a servant of His divine grace. The nuclear-like explosion of the King's Life within your soul will mushroom into a glorious demonstration of God's love and power. *And the result will be a Christ-built man*—the strength of warriors, the inspiration of poets, the wonderment of kings, the playmate of little children, and one of the greatest of God's gifts to women.

How can we resist such an amazing adventure? How can we resist such an amazing opportunity? How can we resist such an amazing God?

The publisher and author would love to hear your comments about this book. *Please contact us at:* www.multnomah.net/ludy

Notes

1. See Job 32.
2. Romans 12:2.
3. Matthew 16:24–26.
4. Matthew 6:24.
5. Melody Green and David Hazzard, *No Compromise* (Chatsworth, CA: Sparrow Press, 1989), 159–164.
6. Matthew 7:15–16.
7. Josef Ton, *Suffering, Martyrdom and Rewards in Heaven* (Wheaton, IL: The Romanian Missionary Society, 1997), 325–326.
8. J. A. Wylie, *History of the Waldenses* (Gallatin, TN: Church History Research and Archives, 1985), 153–159.
9. A. W. Tozer, *The Divine Conquest* (Wheaton, IL: Tyndale House Publishers, Inc., 1995), 145.
10. Ibid.
11. Deuteronomy 30:19–20.
12. Joshua 24:15.
13. Colossians 1:26.
14. Galatians 2:20.
15. 1 Corinthians 6:19–20.

16. Song of Solomon 5:10–16.

17. Tozer, *The Divine Conquest,* 145.

18. Ephesians 6:10–11.

19. Jude 1:3.

20. 2 Timothy 1:14.

21. James 1:27.

22. Ephesians 5:25, 28.

23. Job 31:1, NIV.

24. Philippians 2:3–4.

25. Ezekiel 11:19, NLT.

26. Psalm 34:8, NIV.

27. V. Raymond Edman, *They Found the Secret* (Grand Rapids, MI: Zondervan, 1984), 5.

28. Philippians 3:12–14.

29. 1 Peter 3:7.

30. John 13:14–15.

DISCOVER THE ADVENTURE OF A LIFETIME

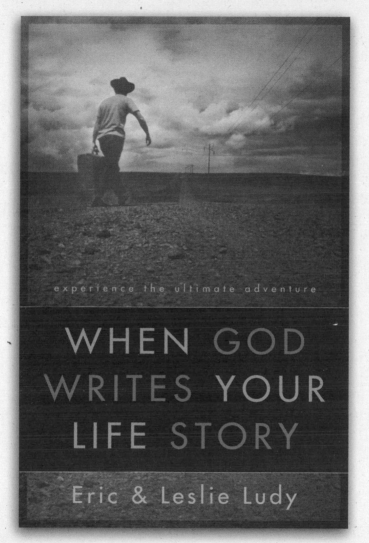

experience the ultimate adventure

WHEN GOD WRITES YOUR LIFE STORY

Eric & Leslie Ludy

Whether you're currently tackling major life decisions or simply longing to live a life that really counts, When God Writes Your Life Story will infuse you with vision and purpose. This book introduces the amazing journey that awaits us when we step into God's endless frontier. It showcases the heroic potential of the true Christian life. The God of the Universe wants to write your life story. And when He does, you mustn't expect a mediocre tale!

FIND ROMANCE IN ITS RICHEST FORM

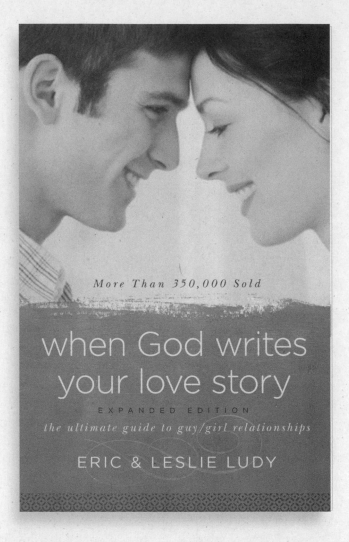

More Than 350,000 Sold

when God writes
your love story

EXPANDED EDITION

the ultimate guide to guy/girl relationships

ERIC & LESLIE LUDY

In their most popular book, bestselling authors Eric and Leslie Ludy challenge singles to take a fresh approach to relationships in a culture where love has been replaced by cheap sensual passion. *When God Writes Your Love Story* shows that God's way to true love brings fulfillment and romance in its purest, richest, and most satisfying form.

WHEN DREAMS
COME TRUE

a love story
only God could write

Eric & Leslie Ludy

This daringly real, intensely moving love story gives vision and hope to everyone in search of a love worth waiting for. In their bestseller *When God Writes Your Love Story*, Eric and Leslie Ludy described the breathtaking perfection of God's plans for each young person and offered fresh guidelines for being Christlike in relationships with the opposite sex. *When Dreams Come True* shares the Ludys' personal story, illustrating how they lived out the principles of the first book in their own romance and marriage.

FIND LOVE THAT NEVER FALLS SHORT

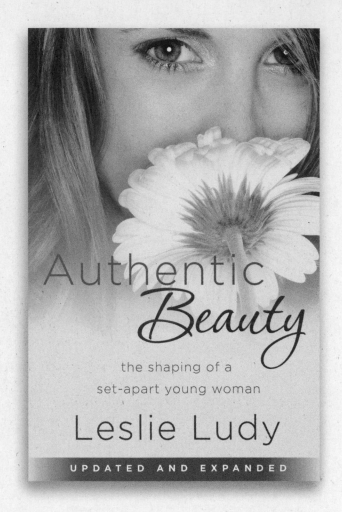

In a world that seeks to destroy all that is princesslike and feminine within her, that mocks her longing for tender romance and exalts the empty charms of a painted face or a perfect figure—can today's young woman dare to long for more? For every young woman who has asked herself that question, this book offers a breathtaking vision of hope. Refreshingly candid and practical, *Authentic Beauty* explores the boundless opportunities God has for a young woman who is willing to let Him shape every aspect of her life.

MUSIC FROM ERIC AND LESLIE LUDY

ISBN 978-1-92912-527-2 $15.99